10 Seconds of Insane Courage fundamentally changed the way I contemplate decisions. It is a must-read for business leaders, entrepreneurs, and anyone making a major decision. Move this book to the top of your reading list now.

    — **Jeff Croft, Microsoft**

Leadership guru, adventurer and Southern gentleman with a touch of Jay Gatsby—Garrett Gravesen *is* Carpe Diem in the flesh! In *10 Seconds of Insane Courage,* readers learn to create their own genius and push beyond their comfort zone. Mr. Gravesen's approach is akin to the teacher who insists students color outside of the lines!

    — **Katherine Pietrantonio, Harvard classmate**

Garrett's honest account of his personal experiences with fear make the topic very approachable for the reader, but what is more impressive is his ability to make the case for courage. Garrett's philosophy on how to live every day to the fullest is laced throughout every page of this book. I realize now that I don't need years, weeks or even days to overcome my fears . . . just 10 seconds of insane courage, and it's worth it.

    — **Sam Konigsberg, Vice President, BlackRock**

There are so many important qualities in life, but Garrett embodies the one that holds so many back from realizing their dreams: courage! From scaling glaciers in Antarctica, to saving children in Africa, to speaking to thousands around the world and countless other examples, Garrett has figured it out. We'd all be wiser to follow the path he lies out in *10 Seconds of Insane Courage.*

    — **Grant Zarzour, MD, Founder, Fuse Project**

Garrett's life is a journey of three very distinct themes: adventure, leadership and humility. Combined, they are the formula for 21st century resiliency, which is why Garrett Gravesen has emerged as the world's foremost leader on both the art and science of courage. As cultures across our world continue to chaotically unravel, Garrett's memoir becomes increasingly timely, necessary and a must-read for all of us who genuinely seek a roadmap to thrive in the 21st century.

    — **Gary Whitehill, Founder, New York Entrepreneur Week, and**
       Chief Futurist, African Union

10 SECONDS OF INSANE COURAGE

HOW TO **UNLOCK** YOUR **COURAGE** TO **UNLEASH** YOUR **POTENTIAL**

GARRETT GRAVESEN

Jacket design by Elena Suster.
Interior design by Anne McLaughlin, Blue Lake Design.

ISBN: 978-1-947505-02-5
Published by Baxter Press, Friendswood, Texas
First printing 2017
Printed in the United States

Publisher's note: To ensure anonymity, some names and details have been changed in many of the stories in this book.

Contents

The Insane

CHAPTER 1

Is Playing It Safe Holding You Back?

The sound of a text message jolted me awake. It was 7:45 A.M.—far too early for any text message, in my opinion. As I rolled over and stared at the screen, I stopped. I rubbed my eyes and read the words on the screen one more time. I realized something was wrong.

I was spending a few days in San Francisco with a friend. We had just gotten back from a fantastic trip to Cuba. I had just co-founded ADDO, a leadership consulting company, with my best friend Kevin Scott, and we had a promising new client. If we could land a couple of other big consulting jobs, we just might make this thing work! My friend in San Francisco was a Harvard Law grad and an executive at Twitter. This guy could open doors Kevin and I had only dreamed about. Life was "moving up and to the right" in a big way, and I was excited about the future.

My Dad knew that I hated getting up early, but it was his message that glared at me from the phone. It was almost 11:00 a.m. in Atlanta where he lived. The short message was something I'd never read before or since: "We need to talk. Call me."

Instantly, I knew there were only two options: Either someone was in big trouble (a car crash, unplanned pregnancy, or death came to mind) or my father had found out something I'd done, and I was in big trouble! Instantly, my memory scanned the past couple of years to see if Dad could have discovered any of the crazy things I'd done. There were too many to count.

Within seconds, my mind went into overdrive, and adrenaline flooded every cell. I called him immediately, but my Aunt Sharon answered. That wasn't a good sign. She lived in Florida, why was she in Atlanta answering Dad's phone? I was now sure the worst had happened. Every second seemed like an eternity before she explained what was going on.

Her first words were, "Give me a couple of seconds to step out into the hall."

Oh great. Was she stepping out of intensive care where my Dad lay near death? Was she already at the funeral home?

She finally began, "We just met with the doctor the second time to get the results of the tests. We just found out your Dad has Stage 4 cancer."

She then went silent. I guess she was letting me process her words, but I wasn't sure what to make of them. I didn't know anything about cancer, so I wasn't sure if there were four or a hundred stages. The context clues told me that Stage 4 wasn't good at all.

Finally, she spoke again: "I know you want to talk to your Dad. We're both pretty upset."

Before she could give the phone to Dad, I asked the one question that immediately came to mind: "How long does he have to live?"

Aunt Sharon paused for a second and then said, almost in a whisper, "They're giving him about a year."

She handed the phone to Dad, and he began, "Garrett, I don't want you to worry. You have a lot of important things going on, and you're all the way across the country. I want you to have a good time with your friends in San Francisco. When you finish your trip, you can come home and we'll talk about all this. We'll figure out what all of this means."

That's my Dad. He just got a death sentence, but he was more concerned about me having a good time and making connections

This phone call either created or awakened a world of fears in me. Maybe they had all been there before but I'd shoved them down below the surface. I don't know where they'd been, but suddenly, they were lions roaring in my face.

My Dad was going to die within a year. All my life I had been able to talk my way into opportunities and out of trouble, but no amount of persuasive words could change this stark fact. I've always been sure I could meet any challenge and inspire people along the way, but this was different. I've always had a knack for finding option C when options A and B don't work. I knew the formula for success: You create something, market it, sell it, and scale it. I'd created non-profits and for-profits. I'd consulted with major companies, and we were on the verge of a major breakthrough in our growth. I'd made a living by creatively solving problems, but none of my talents, wit, or experience could alter the painful truth of this moment. The person who believed in me more than anyone on the planet was going to die, and there wasn't a thing I could do about it. This time, my role wasn't to solve the problem. My only part was to be present and support a dying man I dearly loved.

A hundred times on the flight back, I asked myself, *What in the world am I going to do? I don't know anything about cancer.* My confidence was shattered. I wondered how I could be strong for my father, I doubted my ability to cope with his failing health, I couldn't imagine how I could fulfill all the commitments I'd just made in our new company, I wondered if what I had been pursuing was meaningful at all, and I was terrified by all the things that were out of my control (which suddenly went from a few things to everything). On the long flight back, everything in my life was up for grabs. All of the new and exciting opportunities seemed suddenly and ultimately empty . . . or at least confusing. I faced the cold, hard reality that I was walking into a situation for which I was completely unprepared and incompetent. The future that had seemed so bright now looked like dense fog at night. The entire plane flight was a nightmare of doubt and fear.

People had always seen me as bold, creative, and confident (and I made sure I projected that image everywhere I went), but suddenly I felt overwhelmed, paralyzed, and helpless. My confidence was now only a memory. I was unsure and insecure.

When I walked in the door at my Dad's condo, we hugged each other and wept for a long time. Both of us knew that nothing would ever be the same. Fear became my constant companion.

The fears described in this book are my fears, the ones I've become painfully aware of since that awful day I got the text from my Dad. Maybe you can relate to some of them.

THE CONCEPT OF "10 SECONDS OF INSANE COURAGE"

I had dinner with my friend Lisa Wilson and a few others at a restaurant in Atlanta. As young singles often do, we talked about the importance and the complexity of relationships. At one point, Lisa told us, "Getting into a relationship or getting out of one takes the same thing: it takes 10 seconds of insane courage to say 'yes' or to say 'no more.'" She was getting out of a relationship, and she explained that she really liked the guy, but it just wasn't right. She explained, "I needed 10 seconds of insane courage to tell him it's over. In a moment . . . it was only 10 seconds . . . I knew I just had to speak up and say the first words. If I could find the courage to say the first few words, the rest would follow. And that's exactly what happened."

Instantly, I realized the principle applies to every aspect of life, not just dating. I told her, "That's one of the most profound things I've ever heard in my life."

Lisa laughed, "Great! Take it. It's all yours."[1]

People need 10 seconds of insane courage to make all kinds of decisions in dating, marriage, raising kids, their career, hobbies, travel, and every conceivable adventure. Here are a few:

- asking for a raise
- asking someone on a date
- pitching a new product
- raising your hand and speaking up in a meeting
- taking the job and moving away
- asking that person to marry you
- saying "yes" or saying "no, it's not right"
- speaking up to the boss when you have something important to say
- being vulnerable with your spouse about something you did
- leaving work to spend time with your kids
- listening to hard truth
- jumping out of a plane to skydive
- applying for a new job
- giving a speech
- buying the plane ticket to go where you've never been before
- saying goodbye
- introducing yourself to someone "out of your league"
- offering your time when someone is lost and needs help
- and countless more

In those 10 seconds, everything in you screams, "Don't do it!" In that moment, you'll remember a dozen reasons why it's a bad idea, and you'll probably think of a dozen new excuses to back away from the ledge. Every ounce of reason and every drop of emotion will scream at you to stop. That's why it takes "insane courage." In that precise moment, you have to find the will to punch in the phone number, raise your hand, and say the first words of the first sentence. And have the confidence that the rest will follow.

People who play it safe live with regrets. One act of caving in to fear leads to another, and then self-doubt says, "You couldn't have done it anyway." Soon, the downward spiral of shame erodes any semblance of confidence, and living with fear becomes a tragic normal. Passion and drive that once existed begin to dwindle, and only emptiness remains. These people endure unlived lives. They settle for less—and they know it. Of course, we need 10 seconds of insane courage to jump out of an airplane or swim with sharks, but I want to focus on having the guts to do something bold in *countless everyday events*, as well as a few more dramatic moments when courage is required.

Each of us is born for a purpose, and we want our lives to matter. I don't think it's unique to only some of us; it's a longing of every human being. Yes, we live with very real fears and feelings of inadequacy, but we long for our lives to be bigger, better, and bolder. We want to make a difference. Somewhere in the depths of our souls, we know we're born for more.

Too often, though, we feel stuck, and we need a gentle push . . . or maybe a kick . . . to act in those 10 seconds. I'd be the first person to tell you that no one is courageous on their own. We soak up the attitudes of those around us, for good or bad. To become bold people who strive to make a difference, we need a "circle of conspirators": people who have a track record of courage . . . people who care enough to tell us the truth . . . people who won't settle for us staying stuck any longer. We don't need a dozen of these people, but we desperately need one or two.

In *The 2 AM Principle*, author John Levy quotes his mentor, "The quality of our lives is defined by the people we surround ourselves with and the conversations we have with them." Then Levy explains, "The importance of this lesson is that an exceptional life is about curating the people around you. Most people end up with friends based on proximity and coincidence. They went to the same class, worked at the same company, or lived in the same building. These may be lovely and wonderful people, but the true opportunity comes from seeking out people because we admire their character, attitude, and skills."[2]

Every time I have taken a big step in my 10 seconds of insane courage, a few close people—particularly my parents, my brother Jeff and his wife Becca, my close friends Kevin Scott and Jon Vaughan, as well as others outside my circle that I've encountered in my work and on my travels—have encouraged me, listened to my doubts, prompted me to take the plunge, and picked me up when I fell. At every point, they weren't surprised when I admitted I was scared to death to take the next step, and I wasn't surprised when they never wavered in their support. All of them have pushed me one step farther to live bigger, better, and bolder.

In many ways, I hope the stories in this book (mine and the ones about many other people) are a type of "virtual support system" to inspire you in your 10 seconds when you need insane courage. If you feel afraid, we've felt afraid. If you want to quit, we've wanted to quit. If you have excuses, we've had plenty of them, too. So, as you read this book, you can be sure you aren't the only one who feels like caving in and running away from your fears. Face them anyway.

EVERYTHING YOU WANT

IS ON THE OTHER SIDE OF FEAR.

—Jack Canfield

CHAPTER 2

Digging Deeper

Courage isn't the absence of fear; it's the willingness to push through it. Psychologist Rollo May identifies two distinct kinds of fear. One is good and productive. It's specific, targeted, and limited to a single experience, like seeing a speeding car headed toward you. It kicks the autonomic nervous system into gear, and an adrenaline rush enables you to act quickly to get out of the way.

The other kind is what he calls "anxiety." It may have begun with a healthy fear, but the residue of fear doesn't subside after the event. It lingers and turns toxic . . . or corrosive . . . leaving the autonomic nervous system "on" all the time.[3] To cope with these persistent, nagging feelings, we find ways to manage the fear by hiding from perceived threats, medicating the feelings, or attacking those who bother us. None of these avenues actually addresses the underlying problem. In fact, they multiply our unhealthy fears.

For most of us, the healthy and unhealthy fears tend to overlap. The fears that hold us back may have begun when we were genuinely threatened and scared out of our minds, but for some reason, our alarm system didn't go back to normal. The sense of being threatened remained, and it has become a familiar (and unwelcome) part of our daily lives. In fact, we've become so used to it that we don't even notice it any longer.

In this book, we will look at 8 Fear Factors. I've wrestled with all of them at one time or another. My guess is that you will easily identify one or two of them lurking in the recesses of your thoughts. Read the whole book, but camp out in those chapters. I hope you identify one Fear Factor that is truly holding you back, and you never forget what you read, the examples of those who struggled through it, and the timeless tips, tactics, and techniques to overcome your fear and set you free to live the life you were made for. Let's jump in.

The 8 Fear Factors include:

- Fear Factor 1: Fear of the unknown
- Fear Factor 2: Fear of letting go
- Fear Factor 3: Fear that I'm not good enough
- Fear Factor 4: Fear of the first step
- Fear Factor 5: Fear of bailing out
- Fear Factor 6: Fear of not having enough
- Fear Factor 7: Fear of disappointing others
- Fear Factor 8: Fear of failure

Creative Diversions

We are incredibly creative in coming up with reasons we avoid speaking up and making bold choices in our most important relationships and at work. Do any of these statements sound familiar?

We hide:

> "I don't know what to do."
>
> "It's best to play it safe."
>
> "Nobody thinks I have anything to offer."
>
> "I'm not very creative."
>
> "It's not my job to come up with new ideas."

We give in:

> "It's easier to go with the flow."
>
> "I'll just go with it."
>
> "Other people know a lot more than I do."
>
> "The risk of honesty is just too high for me."
>
> "That's not a mountain I want to die on . . . or even fight on."

We criticize:

> "That'll never work."
>
> "If this is a good idea, why hasn't anyone done it before?"
>
> "They haven't even thought through it all."
>
> "Where's the data? Where's the research?"
>
> "Creative people never really get work done."

THIS CUTS DEEP

Let's start with a brief philosophical and psychological description. The 8 Fear Factors described in the chapters of this book aren't just temporary emotions. They are deeply held beliefs, the way we see people and events, a perception of reality that may be severely limiting and harmful but seems completely good, right, and normal. When I talk about the 8 Fear Factors, I've noticed two opposite responses in most individuals: first, they desperately want to overcome their fears and live with courage, joy, and freedom, but second, they fiercely resist the necessary changes. This combination leaves them longing for more but stuck in their cherished (but often faulty) beliefs about themselves, other people, and opportunities.

Modern psychology uses many different templates to explain how people get stuck in their controlling perceptions and how they can change. One of the clearest and most powerful models to help people overcome their fears is "schema therapy," which identifies the destructive, powerful beliefs as "lifetraps."[4]

In their book, *Reinventing Your Life*, authors Young and Klesko explain, "Schemas are deeply entrenched beliefs about ourselves and the world, learned early in life. These schemas are central to our sense of self. To give up our belief in a schema would be to surrender the security of knowing who we are and what the world is like; therefore, we cling to it, even when it hurts us. These early beliefs provide us with a sense of predictability and certainty; they are comfortable and familiar. In an odd sense, they make us feel at home. This is why cognitive psychologists believe schemas, or lifetraps, are so difficult to change."[5]

This explanation makes us ask: *Is it possible to overcome deeply rooted beliefs about the way life works? Can we find a new source of courage where there had only been fear and self-doubt?* The answer is, Yes. That's what this book is all about.

If we want to climb higher and live more fully, we have to dig deeper, uncover our fears, face them with astounding courage, and take the hardest and most necessary steps we've ever taken. No matter how hard it is in those 10 seconds, your choice of insane courage will radically change your life. Truly.

Now, let's dive into the 8 Fear Factors.

ONE ISN'T NECESSARILY BORN WITH COURAGE, BUT

ONE IS BORN WITH POTENTIAL. WITHOUT COURAGE,

WE CANNOT PRACTICE ANY OTHER VIRTUE WITH

CONSISTENCY. WE CAN'T BE KIND, TRUE, MERCIFUL,

GENEROUS, OR HONEST.

—*Maya Angelou*

FEAR FACTOR 1

Fear of the Unknown: *What's Behind Door #3?*

**FEAR SAYS,
"YOU DON'T KNOW WHAT YOU'RE GETTING INTO."**

**COURAGE RESPONDS,
"YOU DON'T KNOW WHAT YOU'RE MISSING OUT ON!"**

CHAPTER 3

Paralyzed

Actor Will Smith recommends all of us to schedule a daily confrontation with our fear. "The problem," he observes, "is that fear lies." He explains that facing his fears became a daily practice after he made his first skydive in Dubai. Smith said it often works like this: You're out at dinner or at a bar with your friends, and one of them says, "Hey, we should go skydiving tomorrow." You and all your friends yell, "Oh yeah" and give each other high fives. Then, when you get back to your hotel room, you think about what you've made a commitment to do. You come up with all kinds of excuses why this is the dumbest idea in the history of the world, and thoughts of actually jumping out of an airplane several miles up in the sky make you shudder. You don't sleep. You can't sleep. All night, you hope your friends don't remember talking about skydiving.

Then the sun comes up. You show up where you all agreed to meet, just in case, and everybody is there. Great. All of you are acting excited and pumped up . . . even you. It's all an act. On the drive over to the airfield, your stomach is in knots, and you hope it stays in knots and doesn't explode. That would be ugly.

At the airfield, some macho guy gives the safety brief. He talks about what happens if the parachute doesn't open. Great. That helps a lot. For the first jump, you're harnessed to one of the instructors. When you get on the plane, you sit in that guy's lap. Yeah, it's awkward, but there are more important things to worry about. To check him out, Smith says he asked the guy, "So you have kids, right? You've got people you need to see after this is over?"

As the plane climbs to 14,000 feet, Smith noticed a set of lights near the door. All the time the plane is climbing, the light is red. But he realized at some point the yellow light will come on . . . and then the green one. When that happened, somebody opened the door. "And in that moment, you realize you've never been in a fricking plane with the door open. Terror. Terror. Terror."

A couple of friends go first. They vanish when they jump out the door. Then, it's your turn. Your guy walks you out to the door, and your toes are on the edge of oblivion. "You're looking out down at death." The instructor yells over the noise of the wind, "We're going on three." He counts, "One . . . two" and then he pushes you out the door. He knows that if he got to three, you'd grab the sides of the door and hang on for dear life.

"In one second, you realize it's the most blissful experience of your life. You're flying! And you realize there is zero fear. The point of maximum danger is the point of minimum fear. It's bliss!"

Smith asks himself, "Why were you scared in your bed the night before? Why were you scared in the car? Why couldn't you enjoy breakfast? Up to the point of jumping out of the airplane, there's no reason to be scared. It only ruins your day. And in that moment when you should be terrified, it's the most blissful experience of your life."

He draws this conclusion: "God placed the best things in life on the other side of terror. On the other side of your maximum fear are all of the best things in life."[6]

LAME . . . BUT THEY SOUND SO REASONABLE

Excuses are the default mode of the human heart. They're certainly mine. We claim to be confused so we won't have to make hard choices: When we don't know, we don't do. When we can't guarantee a predicted outcome, we become paralyzed by indecision, which is what fear looks like when we face the unknown.

Most of us have vivid imaginations. We contemplate a negative outcome, and then we blow it up to incredible (and incredibly horrid) proportions. It won't just be bad; it'll be catastrophic! The conversation or event we're thinking about is, in reality, only Nemo, but in our minds, it's a great white shark.

WHAT IF?

Many of us live with a negative assumption about the answer to "What if . . . ?" Our thoughts spiral downward to "What if this terrible thing happens? What will happen to me, to this relationship, or to my career?"

It's good to be wise and prudent. It's smart to ask good questions before you take a step, but this fear is way beyond that. If we haven't read the playbook before, it's easy to assume the worst. If we've tried before and been hurt by someone we love, we can't imagine trying and feeling that awful rejection again. If we've tried before and failed, that failure becomes the defining "truth" that crushes every hope and desire in our hearts. We're certain, though, this is the only truth. There is no other. So our excuses sound completely logical and they feel completely right.

We've seen what's behind Door #1 and Door #2. These are the obvious two options in any scenario. They may not be attractive, and they may even be dull or harmful, but at least they're known entities. The mystery behind Door #3 terrifies us. We're sure the only plausible outcome of choosing Door #3 is a disaster. Oh, we may have fleeting thoughts that it could actually be something great, but our self-doubt, fear, and shame quickly obliterate this little shred of hope. Many people don't even allow for the brief thought that something good might be behind Door #3. The monster in their memory is too big, too mean, too cruel to allow for any hope for something better. They believe they don't deserve it. They believe they can never have it.

Familiar Excuses

We all have our insecurities that manifest themselves in fears that sound like excuses. Here are some of the excuses I've heard (or said) to avoid the unknowns behind Door #3:

"I just need more information."

"Because I don't know it, I don't do it."

"I can't stand anything uncertain, unpredictable, or out of my control."

"I can't control it, so I won't go for it."

"I can't ask her out. She'll laugh at me."

"I can't go out with him. He's too . . ."

"I can't take that job. I don't know anyone there."

"Uncertainty terrifies me."

"If I don't know the end of the story, I won't read the first page."

"What if I fail?"

"What if I actually succeed? The pressure on me will be enormous from that point on."

"I just know something really bad is going to happen. I can feel it."

"What if I go broke and become homeless . . . or have to move back in with my parents?"

Does it help to identify these thoughts and feelings? Absolutely. Holding them up to the light is the first step in overcoming them. In fact, if you can't see them, hear them, and feel them, you have no hope of addressing them.

CHANGE IS HARD BECAUSE PEOPLE OVERESTIMATE THE VALUE OF WHAT THEY HAVE—AND UNDERESTIMATE THE VALUE OF WHAT THEY MAY GAIN BY GIVING THAT UP.

—*James Belasco and Ralph Stayer*

CHAPTER 4

The Illusion of Control

Here's the truth: No matter how hard you try, you can't control everything. One of the marks of healthy people is the ability to discern what they control and what they don't . . . and feeling okay about the inevitable unknowns in life. In reality, those who struggle with this fear probably have much more control than they realize. The paradox is that realizing we can't control everything gives us freedom, power, and wisdom to control more of our lives.

You know more than you think you know. You have more wisdom than you assume you have. You have more abilities than you think you possess. When you realize these truths, you have more control over your decisions and the outcomes than you ever imagined.

FEAR AND TRUTH

When our fear dominates our thoughts, we assume, "I'll start, I'll fail miserably, and it'll be a stain on my reputation for the rest of my life." When the truth is far more likely to be: "I'll start, progress will be messy, success may be different than I imagined, and I'll learn valuable lessons all along the way." These two mental constructs are worlds apart.

From all of my reading, research, and speaking to successful people, I think this truth is universal: Every successful person has faced enormous unknowns, but they found enough courage to take the leap and give their idea a shot. Invariably, they failed many times along the way. They faced setbacks, doubts, criticism, and insecurity, but they still had control over their decisions, and they chose to keep moving forward. Plenty of people warned them, "You don't know what you're getting into," but they responded (at least enough times to keep some momentum), "Yeah, but I don't want to miss out on something great." Failure was always part of the pavement on the road to greater success.

I've also talked to many men and women near the end of their lives, and almost without exception, they've told me, "Garrett, I wish I'd taken more risks when I was younger. I wish I hadn't played it so safe. I had some big ideas, some great opportunities, but I chose a predictable path . . . too predictable." Some of them confided, "To be honest, many of my worst fears never came true. And if they did, I could have handled them. I missed out on far too much. I wish I'd gone for it."

40 YEARS AND 30 DAYS

My Dad worked in the insurance business for 40 years. 30 days after retiring, he found out he had Stage 4 cancer and a year left to live. Far too often, life isn't fair. He told me he had put off travel and adventure and following his passions in hopes that he would have plenty of time later for those pursuits. Over his career, Dad thought many times about changing professions. He had other ideas, other goals, and other dreams. But Door #1 felt safe and secure, so he kept choosing it. The reason Dad always encouraged me to go for broke was that he wanted me to live a full life. Now. He enjoyed experiencing these things vicariously through me. He didn't verbalize it in this way, but his attitude toward me was always, "I may not try new things, and I may not take these risks, but you sure should!" It was always that encouragement that kept me going.

All we have is today, but that's enough. How can we open a new door in this moment, at this point in our lives, whether we're young or old?

PREDICTABILITY COMES WITH A PRICE

Yes, we instantly think of a zillion excuses. Those are, as we've seen, our default mode. But there's a life to be lived behind Door #3—a more exciting life. It's a riskier life for sure, but one that offers at least a measure of excitement as we plunge into something that doesn't have a guaranteed outcome. People at every stage in life have their own set of excuses: in college, as young singles, just married, starting a career, with a mortgage and kids, in a stable career, nearing retirement, and after retirement. There are plenty of reasons to choose the first two doors, but predictability comes with a price—soul-numbing sameness.

Don't misunderstand me. I'm not saying we should all choose the most ridiculous risks we can imagine, but we can listen to the voice that tells us, "Try this. Imagine that. Go for it and see what happens." Most of those choices happen in the context of what we're already doing. We just become more alive and creative as we do them. But sometimes, our dream is to do something radically different.

Do you hear the voice inviting you to open Door #3—a new unexplored option? Some of us have neglected it so long, or we've endured such traumatic experiences, that we've refused to listen for it any more. But it's there. If you're alive, it's there. The voice is there. Listen for it. Listen to it. And no, there are no guarantees that the voice will lead us instantly and smoothly to success after success. There will be plenty of twists and turns on the journey. If you want guarantees, stay with what's safe. If you want to really live, open Door #3.

People who have listened to the voice and answered the call are the best storytellers and most interesting people in the world. Why? Because every Door #3 produces stories of adventure, road-blocks, encounters with strangers, and the best friends they ever had. And these people can't wait to tell you about it. Were they afraid when they started? Absolutely. They'll tell you about it. Did they feel overwhelmed by self-doubt when things didn't go well? Certainly. But their eyes light up when they describe the turning points, the people who believed in them, and the outcomes that were better than they ever imagined. These people have great stories, and we can be like them.

Courage Sounds Like This…

"What if not knowing isn't a terrible thing?"

"What if what's behind Door #3 is really Nemo, not the shark?"

"What if I listen more carefully to the voice that tells me to take a risk?"

"What if the road behind the door is the adventure of my life?"

"What if I refuse to take the easy way out?"

"What if I stop living in fear and find the courage to really live?"

POSITIVE WHAT-IFS . . .

Change doesn't happen by wishing. We create change only when we envision a different future and we take action to fulfill it. Too many of us have let our imaginations poison our minds and made us think the unknown is terrifying. Now we need to create new habits of the mind by choosing to dwell on positive "what-ifs." Then, as we become more confident and creative—as we listen to the voice that's confident and creative—we need to take action. We write on a vision board, we create a plan, and we have concrete action steps. We may resist picking up the pen, but at least now we know why we're resistant, and we fight back.

Writing down a goal is a surprisingly powerful practice. A Harvard researcher found that something as simple as a New Year's resolution sharpens our resolve. Francesca Gino observes, "[T]emporal landmarks like the New Year do help motivate us to reach our long-term goals when such goals are salient in our minds. This is because these landmarks trigger reflection and thus can potentially highlight the gap between our current behavior (such as watching TV every night or overspending) and our rosier, desired future behavior (working out every night or saving more). We all regularly face decisions that entail a conflict between choices that primarily provide instant gratification and virtuous ones that mainly provide long-term benefits (watching TV versus working out)."[7]

The simple act of writing activates neurotransmitters in the brain that provide a fresh and strong motivation to take action and use your existing skills. Cut out a picture from a magazine and put it on your desk. Write a slogan on your bathroom window. Put a memento in your wallet or purse to remind you of your goal. It works. Try it. Then write that blog, propose a new product, give that speech, go to that country, lose that weight, set that alarm, raise that hand, speak that truth, or any of a hundred other endeavors your heart continues to whisper.

It's always easier to stay with the familiar, but we come alive when we open Door #3—the door to the unknown. Envision yourself being courageous. Imagine the what-ifs that are positive and hopeful. Write your plans and take action.

When you contemplate taking this step, will you feel scared? Of course. Count on it, but remember what Will Smith said:

GOD PLACED THE BEST THINGS IN LIFE

ON THE OTHER SIDE OF TERROR.

ON THE OTHER SIDE OF YOUR MAXIMUM FEAR

ARE THE BEST THINGS IN LIFE.

CHAPTER 5

The Decision to Jump

What if...? I've asked that question many times. When I was a student at the University of Georgia, I got a scholarship one summer for an internship abroad. I could pick any place in the world, and the university would pay for my plane ticket and housing. I was really excited, but I had never been out of the United States, and I didn't have a passport.

I had a foolproof way to determine my fate. I found a globe. I put my finger on Atlanta, closed my eyes, and spun the globe halfway around. On the opposite side of Planet Earth, I placed my other finger. Seemingly this would be about as far as one could fly on a plane. When I spun the globe back around to see what I had done, I saw that my finger had landed on Hong Kong. It was a far cry from Atlanta, and it promised to be an adventure. I decided at that moment that was where I would go.

I knew nothing about Hong Kong. I didn't know a soul there, and I didn't speak Chinese. Luckily, I discovered many people there speak English. I had no idea how I was going to get an internship in Hong Kong, but I was determined to fly there and figure it out.

In the Atlanta airport, I bought a *Fortune* magazine. The issue listed the "100 Best Companies to Work For." Great. I'd start with those. On the flight over, I read the article and decided how I was going to talk to HR at those companies. (I didn't consider that the list of the 100 best places to work in Hong Kong might be different than the list of American companies.) Upon landing, I googled the HR departments at those companies in Hong Kong and found the ones that had summer internship programs. I made a list of companies and phone numbers. I was ready. This was going to be easy.

It was a disaster. In Hong Kong, I found a cheap room in a dorm at Hong Kong University, and I started going through my list of companies. I didn't want to make too many assumptions, so I started at #100 and worked my way down. I called the first 10. No takers. The next 10. Rejections. The next 10 and the next and the next . . .

I had my local phone and my laptop. Day after day, I called and tried to make contacts to offer my services. In many cases, no one would talk to me. For the others, the barely polite person wasn't interested. It appeared that they might be interested if I'd come from an Ivy League school, but they had never heard of the University of Georgia. (I didn't want to mention our mascot is a Bulldog.) I was running out of the best companies! No one wanted me.

After two weeks of making cold calls for eight hours a day, I was desperate. I'd made an endless number of calls. I'd sent countless emails. I'd called back dozens of times when someone was out. I'd been given numbers of other departments that might help me. Nothing. What was I going to tell the University of Georgia when they asked me how my summer went?

The trajectory of the first two weeks didn't exactly inspire hope. I had to try something else. At that moment, I had an idea that required 10 seconds of insane courage. I decided to be completely, painfully honest with the next person I called. I picked up my phone and called the HR department at Merrill Lynch. The receptionist forwarded me to a lady who said her name was Yulee. I scrapped the opening line I'd been using dozens of times before: "Hi, I'm Garrett Gravesen. I'm calling about the possibility of a 10-week summer internship program with your company." That had gotten me exactly nowhere. Instead, I started with this, "If you'll give me 60 seconds on this phone call, I promise this will be one call you'll never forget for the rest of your life."

She started laughing. Then she told me, "I don't know who you are, but you've already captured my attention."

I jumped in: "I flew 18 hours to a city I found one day on the other side of a globe. I go to the University of Georgia and got a scholarship to come here for the summer. I'm sure you've never heard of it, and that's okay. I don't go to Harvard, Princeton, Yale, Dartmouth, Colombia, MIT, or Stanford. And that's okay as well because we're already on the phone right now. I'm looking for a summer internship program, and you're looking for the best. All I'm asking is to see if you'll have a cup of coffee with me and one conversation in person to hear the rest of my story."

I held my breath for a couple of seconds before she asked with a bit of a laugh, "What is your name again?"

"I'm Garrett Gravesen. I'm here for the entire summer, and I just want to have one cup of coffee. I promise it will at least be interesting."

With yet another laugh she said, "Mr. Gravesen, you may just be in luck. One of our summer interns has decided to work for a consulting firm, so we have one open spot. I can't promise you anything, but I'll have that cup of coffee with you. If it goes well, I'll let you talk to our head recruiter."

Yulee gave me a time to meet her. I didn't have to check my schedule. I was available. I had arrived in Hong Kong with a couple of old suits and a suitcase full of now terribly wrinkled ties. In the previous two weeks, I'd had no occasion to dress up, so they were all still wadded up in my suitcase. I got out my best clothes, ironed them over and over, and tried to look my very best.

When I met with Yulee, I told her the whole story about getting the scholarship, finding Hong Kong on the globe, and trying like crazy to land an internship. I explained, "I've already been turned down 75 times. I wish that wasn't the case, but it *is* true. I know you have students from the best universities around the world. I'm not going to be the smartest intern, but I guarantee you I'll be the hardest working one."

She looked intrigued. I'm sure she'd never had a conversation like this one before. I went for it. "If you'll get me an interview with the recruiter, I promise I won't make you look bad."

Yulee sat back and thought for a few seconds. Then she told me, "Two things. First, did you know we picked all our summer analysts and associates three months ago? In fact, interviews were six months ago. And second, they're flying in next week, and they're all from Ivy League schools."

I smiled and nodded. "No problem. I'll work harder than any of them. I'm already an underdog."

Yulee set up an appointment for me to meet with Merrill Lynch's head recruiter in Hong Kong. I was through one door, but I had another one to open. Brent Robinson was the hiring manager for the summer analyst program that year. He had worked for Merrill Lynch in the U.S., but was transferred to work in the Asia-Pacific region where he did equity research and helped run the summer internship program with American schools. When I walked into his office and told him I was from the University of Georgia, a miracle of biblical proportions occurred: Brent had gone to undergrad at the University of South Carolina. He began by asking me three questions about finance. When he was convinced I knew what I was talking about, we spent the rest of the interview talking about SEC football: the coaches, the players, and the rivalry between his South Carolina Gamecocks and my beloved Georgia Bulldogs.

I could tell he didn't have a lot of people in Hong Kong who could talk to him about one of his primary passions. He then asked how I ended up in his office. From the southern part of the U.S. to the bright lights of East Asia, our stories were vastly different, but our journeys were both incredibly unique. We connected.

Brent offered me the job. It wasn't because of my brains; it was because of my audacity. I understood finance and could work hard, but he said he was more moved by my honesty and sheer willingness to make my own luck. Halfway around the world, we had this in common.

THE UNKNOWN

It took 10 seconds of insane courage to make that call to Merrill Lynch and be brutally honest. Without it, I would have been in that little dorm room with a suitcase full of crumpled clothes for 10 long weeks. I had no guarantees. I only had the hope that opening Door #3, trying the unexpected route, might lead somewhere I wanted to go.

> Fear says, "You don't know what you're getting into."
> Courage responds, "You don't know what you're
> missing out on!"

Yes, it's scary to plunge into the unknown, but it's soul-crushing to refuse to even try. Listen to the voice that invites you to be more, to do more, to dig deeper and climb higher. If you don't hear the voice any longer, think back to a time when you were more eager, more creative, more courageous. Flood your mind with those memories.

Identify Door #3. What is the voice whispering (or shouting)? What do you really want to be and do?

Create a physical manifestation of your dream: a picture on the refrigerator, a vision board, a note in your pocket, a charm or token you carry.

Be completely honest about your fear, your resistance, and your excuses. They are the what-ifs that have held you back. Focus instead on the powerful, positive what-ifs of a better future. Work hard to create a crystal-clear picture of what might happen if you act.

And in those 10 seconds of insane courage, open that door.

IF LIFE WERE PREDICTABLE, IT WOULD CEASE TO BE LIFE, AND BE WITHOUT FLAVOR.

—Eleanor Roosevelt

CHAPTER 6

No Limits

I've met people from all walks of life who, in the course of some pretty soul-baring conversations, have admitted they don't believe they deserve good things to happen to them. Yes, they recognize there is a Door #3, an unknown future, but they're convinced it can only be something bad. These people need to give themselves permission to dream of something good, to envision love and success, to imagine a life they really want to live.

The people who inspire us are invariably people who have stepped into the unknown to take risks. Not everybody takes big risks financially or physically. Some of us take risks relationally and emotionally, putting ourselves out there for someone without knowing how he or she will respond.

Life is full of unknowns. If we run from them, we'll never reach our full potential. If we embrace at least some of them, we'll have more energy, creativity, challenges, and fun than we ever imagined. We'll become people who have great stories.

Permission to try comes with permission to fail, to hit dead-ends, and to not take it personally. Progress always is messy. Can we live with that? Can we accept some messiness in order to really live?

My summer at Merrill Lynch was life-changing, but maybe not in the way anyone expected. I worked 18 hours a day six and a half days a week, and I hated it. The long hours weren't the problem. I hated what I saw the job doing to the people around me. The company expected the interns to work hard, but the career employees worked the same hours. I saw executives who seldom went home to be with their spouses and kids until 10:00 p.m., and they showed up before 7:00 the next morning. I didn't want to forfeit my most important relationships no matter how much prestige and money were attached.

That summer, my 10 seconds of insane courage opened a very important door, but it proved to be one that I never wanted to walk through again. Was that a failure? It depends on how you frame it. I see it as one of the most influential times of my life, one that has shaped my passions, my goals, and my direction. In that way, it was a stunning success.

Sometimes you open that door and you find more than you dreamed, but sometimes you open it and realize it's the wrong path. Regardless, opening the door brings clarity. Opening it teaches lessons that would never have been learned if you'd remained passive and stuck—and you learn them faster. And opening it gives you confidence to open another one. You meet new people, and you have at least one more chapter in the thrilling story of your life.

I HAVE BEEN IMPRESSED WITH THE URGENCY OF DOING.

KNOWING IS NOT ENOUGH; WE MUST APPLY.

BEING WILLING IS NOT ENOUGH; WE MUST DO.

—*Leonardo da Vinci*

10 Seconds Starts Now
ROAD TO COURAGE

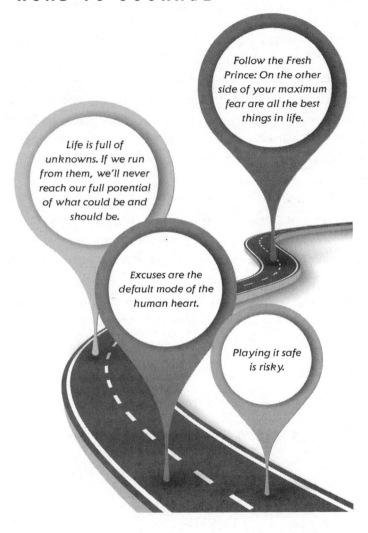

Follow the Fresh Prince: On the other side of your maximum fear are all the best things in life.

Life is full of unknowns. If we run from them, we'll never reach our full potential of what could be and should be.

Excuses are the default mode of the human heart.

Playing it safe is risky.

FEAR SAYS,
"YOU DON'T KNOW WHAT YOU'RE GETTING INTO."

COURAGE RESPONDS,
"YOU DON'T KNOW WHAT YOU'RE MISSING OUT ON!"

FEAR FACTOR 2

Fear of Letting Go: *The Baboon and the Bushman*

**FEAR SAYS,
"PLAY IT SAFE. HANG ON TO WHAT YOU'VE GOT."**

**COURAGE RESPONDS,
"LET GO. LIFE HAPPENS OUTSIDE YOUR COMFORT ZONE."**

CHAPTER 7

The Illusion of Safety

Dave Chappelle walked away from a multi-million-dollar contract for his comedy show at the peak of his popularity. His decision stunned his fans and critics alike. In an interview with Gayle King on *CBS This Morning*, he explained his decision: "I watched one of these nature shows one time, and they were talking about how a Bushman finds water when it's scarce. And they do what's called a salt trap. I didn't know this: apparently, baboons love salt, so they put a lump of salt in a hole in the ground, and they wait for a baboon to come by. The baboon comes, sticks his hand in the hole, and grabs the salt. The salt makes his hand bigger and he's trapped—he can't get his hand out.

Now if the baboon is smart, all he has to do is let go. But he doesn't. He stays there, stuck. The Bushman comes and grabs the baboon, puts it in a cage, and gives it all the salt it wants. It then becomes thirsty. Chappelle continues, "The first place the baboon runs to is water, the Bushman follows him, and they both drink to their fill. In that analogy, I felt like the baboon, but I was smart enough to let go of the salt."[8]

Dave Chappelle was smart enough to realize he was holding on to something really good, but he couldn't have something better until he found the courage to let go of it. I don't think Dave Chappelle is unique. In some way and to some extent, all of us are like the baboon that holds on so tightly to the salt that we can't move and can't grab anything else.

TOO TIGHT

Right now, you already know what you're holding too tightly. It might be a bad habit, or it might be a good habit that has become an unhealthy obsession. It could be a person you're clinging to or a dead-end job that gives you a steady paycheck but nothing else. Some of us can't stop thinking about money, our social media reputation, the next career move, or crazy friends who get us into trouble (but being with them feels so comfortable). The salt in our hands may be obviously destructive or a dream we cherish. No matter what it is, we know we value it too much . . . way too much. It's consuming our lives and preventing us from moving forward. Clinging to it promises safety and security, but it's all an illusion.

My friend Kevin Scott wrote a book called *8 Essential Exchanges.* The subtitle of his book perfectly describes the courage required to let go of the good so we can grab something better: "What you have to give up to go up." Life is a long series of choices. Some are monumental, most are mundane, but they all count. When we choose safety over opportunity—or over freedom or love or adventure or any other risk—we stay trapped in a less meaningful life.

After Gayle King's interview with Dave Chappelle, she sat at the desk with her *CBS This Morning* panel. They were amazed at Chappelle's courage. King commented, "He's very, very thoughtful and very, very smart."

What would Dave Chappelle say about us and our willingness to let go of the good to grab something better? What would Gayle King say about us?

The promised security seems sweeter than sugar and tastier than salt. We don't just want it; we crave it. Safety and security become the driving forces in our lives, and we can't imagine giving them up for any reason.

OUR GREATEST FEAR SHOULD NOT BE OF FAILURE,

BUT OF SUCCEEDING AT THINGS IN LIFE

THAT DON'T REALLY MATTER.

—*Francis Chan*

Living for Safety

What are the statements that prioritize safety over really living? Here are some I've heard (and some I've told myself).

"If I jump, I'll never be able to go back."

"Life's pretty good right now. No need to take any chances."

"Shouldn't I just be okay with where I am?"

"My dreams are unrealistic."

"I don't want to lose what's good even if there's a chance for something great."

"I'll let other people make decisions for me. It's safer that way."

"I don't deserve another chance."

"What if people think I'm a fool for trying?"

"This will never work."

"I don't want anyone to know what's really going on with me. It's better to keep my life a secret."

"I'm a disaster waiting to happen."

CHAPTER 8

Bike Shops and Burning Boats

The practice of "letting go" can be achieved in two very different ways: Gradually and Radically. Both can work really well.

Sometimes, we need to prepare ourselves to let go and do something great. We need to stay where we are and work hard to get ready. Then, when the time is right, we can jump. Wilbur and Orville Wright lived in Dayton, Ohio, at the time the nation and the world found the bicycle to be the latest and greatest invention. When they were boys, their father brought them a toy helicopter made of cork with a bamboo rotor and a rubber band for power. When it broke, they built their own. They realized even as children they had the ability to imagine and create, and flying things captured their imaginations.

THE BIKE SHOP

In 1892, the Wright brothers opened a bike repair and sales shop, and they soon began designing and building their own models of bicycles. Only four years later, three aviation advances caught their attention. Samuel Langley flew a steam-powered, fixed wing aircraft; Octave Chanute and several other engineers tested gliders on the dunes at the shore of Lake Michigan; and later in the year, a man was killed flying a glider. Ironically, this death galvanized Wilbur and Orville's decision to try to design a craft that could safely fly with people on board.

The two brothers spent long hours talking, designing, and testing concepts at night and during all of their free time. But Wilbur and Orville continued running their bike business to have the resources to work on their airplanes. Each year, the brothers continued to perfect their designs in the bike shop and ship their gliders to North Carolina to test them. Each year they continued to work at the bike shop to have the revenue to make more refinements.

Over the next few years, the Wright brothers continued to perfect their airplane designs. They worked at a bike shop to build an airplane. Today we know the Wright brothers because of their airplane, but it was the bike shop that helped them get there. The Wright brothers took the gradual approach, and it still landed them in the pages of history.

BURN THE BOATS!

The other strategy to let go is to make a radical decision. Less than three decades after Columbus discovered the New World, Spanish explorers had probed much of the coasts of North and South America. They wanted gold, and they heard the Aztec Empire was fabulously rich. In 1519, Hernando Cortez led 600 soldiers on eleven ships to the coast of Mexico. They expected to find wealth beyond anything they could imagine, but their force was pitifully small against one of the strongest powers in the hemisphere.

When they landed on the Yucatan, Cortez gave impassioned speeches to his men. He promised riches, but some of the men didn't buy Cortez's promises. They plotted a rebellion and conspired to seize the ships and sail back. Cortez made a decision: Burn the boats.

As the men saw their only escape plan going up in flames, they realized their commander was giving them only two options: conquer or die. Turning back was no longer an option. In one of the most amazing military conquests in history, Cortez and his men captured the emperor Moctezuma at Tenochtitlan, the capital of the Aztecs. Moctezuma was forced to pay vast sums of gold, silver, and precious stones in tribute to the Spanish king.

The radical decision to burn the boats may have made the soldiers wonder about Cortez's sanity at that moment, but his actions forced them to let go of any illusion of safety. They marched and fought like their lives depended on it . . . because they did.

Sometimes, we need to let go of our comfort and invest our afterhours and weekends in our dreams. That's what the Wright brothers did for years, and it paid off. But in other cases, we may realize if we don't do something drastic, we'll never do anything at all. No more dabbling, no more procrastination, no more excuses. If you don't burn the boats, you'll always be looking for the easy way out. It's time to do something definitive. Go for broke.

WE MUST BE WILLING TO LET GO OF THE LIFE

WE'VE PLANNED, SO AS TO HAVE THE LIFE

THAT IS WAITING FOR US.

—*Joseph Campbell*

The Choice to Let Go

Whether it's gradual or radical, we need to tell ourselves some truths:

"Life is meant to be lived."

"If I give in to my fear, I could lose my dream and who I was meant to be."

"I can make my own decisions."

"I'm sure people laughed at every person who has ever taken a risk like this."

"If you're not risking something, you're not really living."

"Confessions from the grave: You can't take it with you."

"I need to let go of the salt and reach for more."

CHAPTER 9

Jump Off the Dock

Nairobi, Kenya . . . not where I imagined I would land after a summer in Hong Kong. The very next summer, I decided not to graduate college. On purpose. I creatively structured my classes and course load to fall one credit short of graduating, and I eagerly pursued one last summer of opportunity. With the extra money I'd saved from Hong Kong, I headed to Kenya—it was an opportunity to experience something far different from the big city and bright lights of a financial capital. I was jumping off the safe dock and into deep water, and I loved it.

Officially, I arrived in Nairobi as part of a student exchange program that provided me with a job, housing, and just enough credibility so my parents didn't lose their minds for a second summer in a row. In reality, I wanted to see how I could serve.

In the middle of May I landed in East Africa in 100-degree heat and a job at a small marketing company. That first week, I looked up volunteer opportunities near where I was living outside of Nairobi. On my first Saturday in the city, I took the twenty-minute bus ride to one of them. I showed up by myself, completely unannounced, at an orphanage. It was scorching hot outside, and 80 children were running around and having a great time on the playground. I ducked into the office to introduce myself with sweat dripping from head to toe. I said I was there for the summer and just wanted to hang out with the kids and see if I could help. The director smiled and nodded. She was really glad to have someone there to volunteer to spend time with the kids.

I went outside. In seconds, sweat was dripping from every pore, but the kids didn't care. They swarmed around me. Their native language is Swahili, but they had picked up pretty good English. One of the little boys stuck to me like glue. His name was Martin. He wore a bright orange shirt and huge, baggy pants. He used his long belt to cinch up his pants so they didn't fall off.

I introduced myself to the children. They had a hard time saying "Garrett" and "Gravesen," so I told them to call me by my initials, GG. It worked! My little buddy Martin was the first one to call out "GG!" and invite me to play. All afternoon, we played on the monkey bars, the jungle gym, the sandbox, and the swing set.

It was a fun afternoon. I was unsure of what would or could happen next. And then something happened. Before I got on the bus, Martin ran up to me. He was ten years old with big brown eyes and a huge smile. He grabbed the bottom of my shirt and tugged on it. He looked me in the eyes and said, "GG, GG, everyone says they'll be back. Will you really come back to see us?"

This little boy, those words, and that moment made me come alive. I knew I'd found a friend, and I'd found my home for the summer: an AIDS orphanage in Nairobi, Kenya. I went to the orphanage every chance I got. After several weeks trying to juggle my work at the marketing company and my trips to the orphanage, I quit juggling and spent virtually all my time with the kids. The execs at the company didn't mind. Days turned into weeks and weeks turned into months. The time flew by. When the summer was over, I couldn't leave. I stayed in Nairobi so I could spend time with Martin and all my little friends at the orphanage. I told my parents that I was going to stay in Nairobi, but I promised I'd come home just before Christmas.

Two weeks before I was scheduled to fly back to Atlanta, Martin's best friend James died of HIV/AIDS. My role with the children, and especially with Martin, had evolved from fun friend to big brother to almost a father figure. The orphanage director asked me to participate in the funeral. That day, we all stood around the grave to honor our friend James. Each of the 80 children put a shovelful of dirt into the grave, saying goodbye their dear friend. I talked about James's amazing life and his love for the others. I was only telling them what they already knew, but I think they were glad to hear it. I prayed for James and for all of us still there. Next to me the entire time was Martin. He held my hand throughout the whole ceremony. All of us were heartbroken, but none more than Martin.

I believe the Good Lord puts certain people in certain places at certain moments for a reason, and I believe I was put there at that moment with Martin.

On my last day at the orphanage, I brought mountains of candy. It was a sweet but sad time with them. As I got ready to get on the bus to leave, Martin came up to me. His big brown eyes looked straight at me. He gave me a high five and a big bear hug. He then said, "GG, GG. You are my favorite friend in the whole world, and I know that best friends keep promises. I want you to promise that you'll always remember me."

I held his hand and said, "Martin, you're my favorite friend, too. I promise, you're one person I'll never forget."

That moment was the inspiration for many of the best things that have happened in my life. He was the inspiration for a charity I later cofounded called H.E.R.O. for Children, dedicated to improving the quality of life of children infected with and affected by HIV/AIDS. And yes, I got to go back and see Martin again years later with a special group of friends and supporters.[9] I've never forgotten Martin, and I never will.

SOMETHING BETTER

I never want to be the baboon trapped because I'm holding too tightly to a handful of salt. I want to be like Dave Chappelle, smart enough to recognize the trap and courageous enough to grab something better. But to grab something better, I had to let go of something good. I had to let go of the expectation that I'd climb a corporate ladder in banking and finance. I had to let go of graduating on time so I could explore my passion of seeing other places and serving other people. I had to let go of any semblance of stability at the marketing company in Nairobi in order to spend more time at the orphanage. I had to let go of the security of working for a major company so I could dive into the crazy dreams of starting a charity straight out of school.

It's a fact of life that we won't let go of what's in our hand until we're convinced something else is tastier, sweeter, or more fulfilling. For me, the image of corporate success, a corner office, plenty of money, and all the perks had been alluring for a long time, but a little boy's question showed me something to live for that was bigger and better.

I think pivotal moments happen for all of us. We just need to notice them and embrace them. In those 10 seconds, we need the courage to let go of the ordinary so we can follow our hearts, do something different, and live out our dream. There are no guarantees everything will work out, but life will be far richer and our stories will be far better. Isn't that worth it?

> Fear says, "Play it safe. Hang on to what you've got."
> Courage responds, "Let go. Life happens outside your comfort zone."

IF YOU ARE NOT WILLING TO RISK THE USUAL,

YOU WILL HAVE TO SETTLE FOR THE ORDINARY.

—*Jim Rohn*

CHAPTER 10

Fully Alive!

What inspires us to face our fear of letting go and find 10 seconds of insane courage to jump? As we've seen, people may respond in two very different but effective ways: itching and burning. First, let's look at the itch.

The Wright brothers didn't close their bike shop when the passion for inventing an airplane gripped them. They didn't burn their boats (or bridges or anything else), but they lived with an irresistible itch to make it happen. Every new idea, whether it succeeded or failed, inflamed their commitment to think harder, be more creative, and try again. For years, they built, repaired, and sold bikes during their normal office hours, but in their spare time, they lived to create a powered airplane that would revolutionize the world!

THE ITCH

Enter my friends Katherine and Craig. Soon after the two got married, they moved to St. Louis. Craig got a job in one of the major accounting firms, and Katherine became a fourth-grade teacher. She loved the kids and thoroughly enjoyed teaching, but in her second and third years at the school, she realized the administration wasn't responding to the needs like she wanted them to. Gradually, in countless conversations with other teachers, friends, and Craig, Katherine developed an itch to become a principal at a school. Then and only then could she implement systems, programs, and relationships she believed were vital for teachers and students. But to become a principal, she needed a master's degree.

For months, Katherine vacillated between optimism and pessimism. She believed she could be a really good principal (other teachers assured her of that), but she didn't want to stop teaching. Besides, she and Craig wanted to start a family. How could she fit all this together?

Katherine looked into a master's program at a university in the city, a program that had two night classes a week and summer intensives. It would take her five years, and it would eat up virtually all of her spare time. She thought about the benefits and the costs, and she decided to go for it.

During the second year of the program, Katherine got pregnant and had a child. Now Craig had to help out even more so she could go to classes and do her homework. And in the fourth year, she had another baby. The pressures were immense, but the itch never went away. Katherine realized her passion to shape an environment in a school was now matched by her joy in creating a loving home for her two children. She finished her degree. The next year, she was accepted for a role as an assistant principal in her school. She's only one step from her goal.

When she looks back on the five long years of study and sacrifice, she shakes her head. "I don't know how I did it. Sometimes, all I could see were deadlines and dead ends, but the itch never went away. I just couldn't let the dream die." Katherine let go of something she enjoyed—her nights and weekends—so she could grab something she longed to do with the rest of her life.

The world of inventions is peppered with people who carved out time and space to scratch their itch to create something new. Here are a few:

- Probably the most famous home invention is the Apple computer created by Steve Jobs and Steve Wozniak in Jobs's childhood home and garage.

- In a garage owned by Susan Wojcicki on Santa Margarita Avenue in Menlo Park, California, Larry Page and Sergey Brin launched Google. Susan needed the money. She had just graduated from business school and needed to pay the month's mortgage.[10]

- Richard T. James was a naval engineer who watched a spring bounce down stacks of books onto the floor. It seemed to have the ability to "walk." He tested a number of different springs until he found just the right combination of flexibility and stiffness. He had invented the Slinky.

There are countless ways to scratch an itch without changing how you make a living or disrupting your life in any significant way. But none of those happen if you aren't aware of the itch and if you don't let it prod you to jump.

AND NOW THE BURN

Most people itch, but a few people burn. Elon Musk knows what it's like to burn the boats and bet it all on a risky venture. He was wildly successful creating and developing PayPal. When it sold, he made $180 million. He decided not to sit back and enjoy his prosperity. He relates his decision, "I put $100 million in SpaceX, $70 million in Tesla, and $10 million in Solar City. I had to borrow money for rent."

Like many new businesses, Tesla had trouble making money. Musk recalls the company was broke. It needed an influx of cash . . . his last cash. He recalls, "Either I went all in, or Tesla dies. I didn't want to look back and say there was something more I could have done and didn't. I spent everything. Everything. I had to borrow money from friends."

Even when his personal finances were bone dry, Musk kept believing in his new space company. Max Levchin, Musk's friend and PayPal partner, described Musk's tenacity: "SpaceX was just a nonstop balls-to-the-wall, doubling- and tripling-down effort. It was him against the odds, swinging the sword in the dark. He gets this crazy vision; he decides to go for it. Things weren't working for him, but he says, 'I don't care. I'll spend another $20 million blowing up another rocket.'"[11]

Burning the boats has worked out for Elon Musk. And sometimes it can work for you!

EITHER WAY WORKS

Gradual or radical—either way works. How do you think the Wright brothers felt that cold December morning when their fragile little plane flew over the sand dunes on the coast of North Carolina? The long hours and long years of scratching their itch paid off. They became pioneers of aviation.

How do you think Katherine felt when she got the job as an assistant principal after five years of scratching her itch by getting a master's degree to qualify to fulfill her dream?

If we're alive, we have a dream. We may have buried it under many years of meaningless work and some instances of heartache, but if our blood still flows, there's a dream down there somewhere. We need to reawaken it, listen to the voice, and feel the itch to do something about it. The vast majority of us aren't going to have articles written about us in *Forbes* or *Fortune*. We aren't wild-eyed entrepreneurs, but our dreams are very real. We may not dream of starting a nonprofit, but of volunteering with one. We may not stop what we're doing to write the great American novel, but we can write a blog, see how people respond, and hone our talents. We may come up with a new idea to implement in our work. To put the pitch together, we may need to stay up late or work on the weekend to perfect it. In this way, we keep earning a paycheck and use every ounce of our creativity at the same time. Do it. We may not leave our jobs to invent a new product, but we can be as creative and persistent as Wilbur and Orville to pursue our dream. It's there. Don't miss it.

HOLDING ON IS BELIEVING THAT THERE'S ONLY A PAST; LETTING GO IS KNOWING THAT THERE'S A FUTURE.

—*Daphne Rose Kingma*

10 Seconds Starts Now
ROAD TO COURAGE

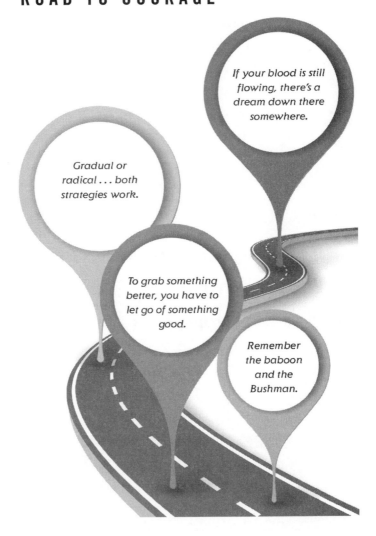

If your blood is still flowing, there's a dream down there somewhere.

Gradual or radical . . . both strategies work.

To grab something better, you have to let go of something good.

Remember the baboon and the Bushman.

FEAR SAYS,
"PLAY IT SAFE. HANG ON TO WHAT YOU'VE GOT."

COURAGE RESPONDS,
"LET GO. LIFE HAPPENS OUTSIDE YOUR COMFORT ZONE."

FEAR FACTOR 3

Fear that I'm Not Good Enough: *Sorry, Superman!*

**FEAR SAYS,
"WHO ARE YOU KIDDING? YOU'LL NEVER SUCCEED."**

**COURAGE RESPONDS,
"IF NOT YOU, THEN WHO?"**

CHAPTER 11

Waiting for Permission

Some of us simply can't pull the trigger on our dreams. It's not that our dreams aren't clear or compelling, and it's not that we're too dense to figure out the next step. Our problem is that in the deepest recesses of our souls, we don't feel worthy or competent or qualified . . . or something. We're waiting for permission to do the thing we were born to do, but we never see the light turn green.

Many of us think we have to be Superman or Wonder Woman, and we feel deficient and defective because we're not. Here's the truth: You don't have to be something or someone you're not. You only need to be yourself . . . and have 10 seconds of insane courage!

One of my favorite people has struggled with the fear of not being good enough. Tragedy and heartache threatened to stop Sheryl Sandberg in her tracks. Her career had been a whirlwind of stunning successes. She graduated *summa cum laude* from Harvard and won the John H. Williams Prize as the top student in her economics class. One of her professors was Larry Summers, who became her mentor. After she graduated, he recruited her to be his research assistant in his new role at the World Bank. She worked with him for a year on projects in India to alleviate leprosy, AIDS, and blindness. Sandberg enrolled in Harvard Business School in 1993 and graduated with highest honors two years later. After receiving her MBA, she became a management consultant for McKinsey & Company before taking another role working for Summers, who was then the Secretary of the Treasury under President Bill Clinton.

When George W. Bush won the White House in 2000, Sheryl left Washington and became the Vice President of Global Online Sales and Operations for Google. She believed Google was going to take off, and she wanted to be part of the journey. In 2007, she met Mark Zuckerberg, CEO of Facebook. The two met again at the World Economic Forum, and Zuckerberg offered her the position of COO. By 2010, Facebook became profitable, and everyone involved became fabulously rich.

In 2013, Sandberg released a groundbreaking book to inspire professional women: *Lean In: Women, Work, and the Will to Lead*. She had become a powerful, positive force in the business world and beyond. However, her world was shaken when she and her husband, Dave Goldberg, were on vacation in Mexico in 2015. Dave had a heart attack and died, leaving Sheryl shocked, grieving, and a single mom raising her children. Honors, degrees, fame, and wealth suddenly meant nothing to her.

Her book about her struggle with grief, *Option B*, was written with a psychologist. She admits she wanted to crawl up in a ball and exit all responsibilities, but she realized she had to give herself permission to go through the dark tunnel of grief so she could eventually come out on the other side. In a *Time* magazine interview, she related, "As a mother you can be heartbroken for yourself but I grew up with a dad and he's still alive. And I'm heartbroken that I was not able to give my children the stability of growing up with two parents, that they lived through and still are living through something so traumatic so young."

The title for the book came from a conversation with good friend Phil Deutch only weeks after the sudden tragedy. Sandberg was upset that she couldn't be at a school event for her son, and she was even more upset that her husband was no longer in her son's life. Deutch put his arm around Sheryl and told her, "Option A is not available. So let's just kick the s--t out of Option B."[12]

If someone as smart, gifted, and experienced as Sheryl Sandberg can hit a wall and wonder if she can get up in the morning and face a new day after a devastating loss, none of us should be surprised by the fear of not measuring up, not making it, not being the success we dreamed of becoming. At some point—almost certainly at several points in our lives—all of us face this fear. You and I aren't Superman or Wonder Woman. We're totally, undeniably human, with all the flaws and foibles endemic to our kind . . . including this daunting fear.

The question isn't whether we should feel the weight of this fear or if we're somehow deficient for being afraid. The question is whether we'll be honest about our insecurities—whether they come from failure, sudden loss, a difficult family background, or any other cause—and find 10 seconds of insane courage to take the next step. We may not have wanted Option B, but it's now the best thing going. Give yourself permission and go.

TRAPPED BY SELF-DOUBT

I've met many people who have all the potential in the world, but they feel trapped by self-doubt. When good things happen, they always ascribe success to other people, circumstances, or luck, but when bad things happen, they take on the full weight of blame: "It's all my fault."

One of my biggest fears is being trapped by self-doubt. I try to keep it hidden, but it's there all the time. When I succeed, I instantly think, "Man, I'm so lucky," or "I'm so fortunate to hang out with such great people." I think about the fact that Coach Dooley (Hall of Fame Football coach and Athletic Director at UGA) has opened so many doors for me, and my friend Kevin has rounded the sharp edges of my personality to make me more effective with executives. Don't get me wrong. I'm not saying we shouldn't be grateful for the ways people have poured into our lives and contributed to our success. We should be tremendously thankful, but we need to have at least a modicum of self-confidence that we have something to offer the people around us.

I'm always overcompensating for the fear of not measuring up. Every speech has to be a little better, every photo needs to be a little more compelling, every conversation needs to be a little more witty or profound. I feel my credentials don't quite cut it, and my performance is always a little less (or a lot less) than it should be. I long for compliments, but I don't believe them when they come. Maybe you have felt this way, too.

I'm driven to stay one step ahead every day, and I'm afraid the world will realize I'm not all that great, or all that smart, or all that gifted. I work hard, and I try to be creative to do a good job, but in the back of my mind, I often wonder, "Do I really know what I'm doing?"

You'd think success would relieve this fear and give far more confidence, but I've found security to be fleeting. With many people, each success only raises the bar, adding more critical eyes, and making people wonder even more if they have what it takes.

"Not Good Enough"

Here are some of the statements I've said and I've heard people say (and undoubtedly, they are even more brutal in their own self-talk):

"I don't have what it takes."

"I'm too dumb to make it on my own."

"I can't do anything right."

"I'll just screw it up."

"I don't have what it takes."

"I'm not an entrepreneur or a risk taker or creative."

"I'm not as good [or smart or talented or good-looking] as him (or her)."

"I just need a real job."

"If people really knew me, they'd laugh at me."

"I deserve all the criticism I get."

"I live with a lot of secrets. If people knew . . ."

"I wear masks all the time to hide who I really am."

"I'm very critical of everybody and everything."

"I'd better not get too close to people. I'd better not let them know who I really am."

I'm not the only one who feels this way. I'm not the only one who lives under a cloud of self-doubt. Years ago in an interview with *Vanity Fair* magazine, Madonna admitted she wrestled with her fear of not being good enough. She told the journalist, "I wish I hadn't done a lot of things, but, on the other hand, if I hadn't I wouldn't be here. But, then again, nobody works the way I work. I have an iron will. And all of my will has always been to conquer some horrible feeling of inadequacy. I'm always struggling with that fear. I push past one spell of it and discover myself as a special human being and then I get to another stage and think I'm mediocre and uninteresting. And I find a way to get myself out of that. Again and again. My drive in life is from this horrible fear of being mediocre. And that's always pushing me, pushing me. Because even though I've become Somebody, I still have to prove that Somebody. My struggle has never ended and it probably never will."[13]

For many of us, *the fear beneath all fears* is the fear of not being enough, not measuring up, not receiving the affirmation we long to hear. This is the fear that drives us and wastes us, the fear that is with us every moment of every day whether we realize it or not. But we can't overcome it if we don't recognize it's there.

THERE WILL BE VERY FEW OCCASIONS WHEN YOU ARE ABSOLUTELY CERTAIN ABOUT ANYTHING. YOU WILL CONSISTENTLY BE CALLED UPON TO MAKE DECISIONS WITH LIMITED INFORMATION. THAT BEING THE CASE, YOUR GOAL SHOULD NOT BE TO ELIMINATE UNCERTAINTY. INSTEAD, YOU MUST DEVELOP THE ART OF BEING CLEAR IN THE FACE OF UNCERTAINTY.

—Andy Stanley

CHAPTER 12

But What If You Can Fly?

B rad Cohen applied to teach at 24 elementary schools, but he received 24 rejections. He hand-carried his résumé to the next school on his list, and this time, the principal saw potential the others hadn't noticed. When he was a child, Brad had been diagnosed with Tourette Syndrome, a disorder characterized by uncontrollable verbalizations, like barking sounds, and sudden movements, such as facial tics and head jerks. Administrators at the previous schools tried to keep a straight face when they met him, but they laughed when he walked out the door. However, a speech therapist at Mountain View Elementary School in Cobb County, Georgia, told her principal, "His résumé is outstanding. What do we have to lose?"

In an interview, the principal asked Brad about his philosophy of teaching and his experience. Brad recalls, "At the end of the interview, they were able to look past my Tourette Syndrome and hire me as a second-grade teacher. I was ecstatic! The dream was right in front of me. It was time. It was showtime!"

Brad won Georgia's award as First Class Teacher of the Year— undoubtedly, to the utter shock of the 24 principals who had turned him down. He had become the teacher he always wanted as a child, but had never had. He recalls, "What makes me a little different from the other teachers is that I have a little bit of insight about the way kids think. I feel like I'm still like a kid, and some kids have disabilities or weaknesses that make them feel a little bit different. I'm able to be a role model they've never had to show them they can overcome their weakness or disability and become successful."

Brad has become a spokesperson for people with Tourette Syndrome, training teachers and serving community associations. When he speaks, he doesn't defend, hide, or excuse the evidences of Tourette. He openly describes his barking and other sounds, as well as the movements of his eyes, face, and head. "The first lesson in the classroom," he explains, "is that people are different. Their teacher has Tourette Syndrome, and he's going to make noises and funny faces all day." He gives his students and those who attend his presentations the opportunity to ask questions—any questions—they want to ask. There isn't a shred of shame in his answers. He jokes as he tells his class, "There's one thing we'll never do, and that's play hide-and-go-seek, because I always lose!"

Brad has learned to appreciate how his disability has proven to be an advantage: "Tourette Syndrome definitely makes me special. If there was a magic potion that could get rid of Tourette tomorrow and I could be like every other teacher, I would say 'no.' Tourette Syndrome has made me who I am."[14]

What does it mean to give yourself permission to be yourself, to stop beating yourself up, and chase your dreams? I think there are several parts to that answer. The most important one is to find at least one person you can trust so you can take off your mask and be completely honest about your fear of not measuring up. With this person, there are no more games, no more manipulation and lies . . . just raw honesty. Oh, I know. This is terrifying. It's the one thing we want more than anything else, but it's also the one thing that scares us most.

IMPARTED OR EARNED

A person's self-concept can be either imparted or earned. If it's imparted by a loving, honest, wise, strong person, we gradually accept the message that we're valuable—at least to one person! This person values us whether we're witty or dense, successful or failing, good-looking or plain. Gradually, very gradually, we begin to believe what that person believes about us. As we become more secure and confident, we give ourselves permission to be flawed, permission to fail, and with it, permission to try something bold and new. We learn to fly!

But if we haven't had or don't have that person with that message to speak to the core of our identity, our only option is to earn an identity by our performance . . . but there's a catch: no matter how well we perform, it's never enough. We're always on a treadmill of trying to measure up, succeeding often enough to keep the promise alive, but secretly afraid we can't really cut it.

Perfection, or the image of perfection, is a terrible burden to carry. Some people are crushed quickly under that weight, but others last a long time trying to prove themselves. The stress gets to most of us sooner or later, and we crash. It's far better to admit that we're broken and limited but still valued and loved. We have talents, we have passions, and with a profound blend of realism and hope, we find the courage to take a risk.

For the vast majority of us, confidence doesn't happen in a flash. It's an acquired trait that is developed only as we fiercely challenge the old, negative assumptions and replace them with the confidence our friend or mentor has instilled in us. In the natural world, growth happens *gradually* and *internally*, but then *visibly* and *inevitably* as we stay connected to the source of our new way of thinking about ourselves and our opportunities.

Let's be honest: it's more comfortable to hide behind our masks than spend time with people who might tell us (or at least show us) we're phony. We need a shot of courage to open our hearts to someone who doesn't play games . . . and who doesn't buy the image we're trying to project. When we hang around an authentic person, we become more authentic, and then we can have the same kind of influence on at least one other person. It's a life-changer. We may be initially amazed at people who present themselves as having it all together, but the wise ones among us are rightly skeptical of those who try to look perfect. As we become more secure and confident, we begin to value those who have taken off their masks and feel comfortable in their own skins. They're rare, but they're out there.

So, find one person who is more authentic than you, and hang out until that person's honesty, courage, and confidence filter into your life. Then, with a new shot of confidence, give yourself permission to fly.

ALWAYS REMEMBER YOU ARE BRAVER THAN

YOU BELIEVE, STRONGER THAN YOU SEEM,

AND SMARTER THAN YOU THINK.

—Christopher Robin

Better Messages

As that one person imparts a new sense of value to us and we become more confident, our self-talk changes. We begin to tell ourselves:

"Failure and fear don't define me."

"I don't have to earn my value anymore."

"I have some real strengths."

"I can be honest and vulnerable with at least a few people, and they'll still love me."

"I can find at least one safe person so I can be myself."

"I need to uncover the source of my gnawing self-doubt and overcome it."

"All of my experiences have prepared me for something great."

"Perfection is an illusion."

"Masks are a false sense of safety."

"If I become real and confident, maybe I can impart that to at least one other person."

CHAPTER 13

Confidence to Jump

Whether we face opportunities or heartbreaks, there's no question that it's a risk to be vulnerable with someone. When we have the courage to take off our masks, we hope and pray the person won't be offended, laugh, or run for the hills, but until we respond with 10 seconds of insane courage, we don't know for sure. The only way to have authentic relationships, though, is to jump into them with honesty and wisdom.

Two people have been incredibly supportive of me in this area: my Dad and Kevin Scott. My business partner Kevin is my best friend. He's been with me in every conceivable high and low, and he's been totally consistent in speaking the truth to me, correcting my faulty thinking, and championing me when I have the guts to try something new. I trust him completely.

I write leadership curriculum and give speeches for a living. That worked really well until I had to speak at my Dad's funeral. After I wrote my message, I gave it to only one person to receive feedback: Kevin. I expected him to tell me to tweak a couple of parts of it, but that's not what he said. After he read it, he said, "Garrett, you could have written this for anyone's father. Delete it and start over. Write it for your Dad."

It was the most heartbreaking and best advice I've ever received. I hit control, copy, alt, delete, and I started over. When I started over, I wrote one word at the top of the page: *Authentic.* As I rewrote, I remembered a standing joke between my Dad and me. He always talked about a day in the future when I would "settle down and get married." I think he looked forward to that day at least as much as I did. Near the end, I told him, "Dad, I don't know if I'll get married within the next year, but I want you, or at least your voice, to be present at my wedding. Would you write a letter to be read at my rehearsal dinner to me and my future wife?"

I wrote this conversation into the speech for my Dad's funeral, but first, I wanted to give the letter some context. At the funeral, I said, "Dad always lived by a principle: 'Trade I for You.' During our last nine months, we went through a book together. It asked some great questions, like: 'What advice would you give to my kid on his first day of kindergarten?' and 'What does being a great father mean to you?' But one question stopped me in my tracks. It simply said: 'What is your greatest accomplishment?' Without even hesitating, he looked at me and said, 'You. You are my greatest accomplishment.' It made me realize he poured his life into me, into something and someone who would outlast and outlive him. He was always trading 'I for You.'"

I told the people at the funeral about asking Dad to write the letter to be read at my rehearsal dinner: "A few weeks ago we were told by hospice care that our time was coming to a close. Dad would always ask if there was anything that I needed, anything left to ask or anything left unsaid—and there was always one thing. Every father wants to be there for his son's wedding day. I didn't make it happen in time. But I really wanted him to be a part of it—one day, with one special woman. And so, with all the courage I could muster, I asked my Dad for one final thing, to write the toast for my future wedding. He cried, I cried, and he said he would do it. It took him three days with a shaky hand and yellow pad of paper, but he did it, and it was the last thing he ever wrote. And now he will be part of that special day with me. Because he wrote it for me . . . and for her."

I took the letter of my pocket to show them. I said, "Someday, I hope I'll get married. At the rehearsal dinner, I'll ask Kevin to read it. I'll be too emotional. It will mean so much. It already does."

After the funeral, someone said, "Garrett, that's the most vulnerable, honest, authentic thing I've ever heard you say. Thank you for being real. Your Dad would be so proud of you today."

If it weren't for Kevin, I would have missed that moment. I had wanted to be strong, to be Superman, but my words that important day would have been stale and flat. Kevin cared enough to tell me the truth and bring out the best in me. I'm so grateful to him for that.

All of us need permission to be real . . . with our most cherished dreams and our most painful insecurities. But quite often, we need someone to step into our lives to give us that permission. I needed Kevin before my Dad's funeral, and Sheryl Sandberg needed friends like Phil Deutch to help her see that giving up wasn't an option. Each person had to admit flaws, failures, and heartaches, but each one also realized 10 seconds of insane courage was worth the risk.

> Fear says, "Who are you kidding? You'll never succeed."
> Courage responds, "If not you, then who?"

WE NEED PEOPLE IN OUR LIVES WITH WHOM WE CAN BE AS OPEN AS POSSIBLE. TO HAVE REAL CONVERSATIONS WITH PEOPLE MAY SEEM LIKE SUCH A SIMPLE, OBVIOUS SUGGESTION, BUT IT INVOLVES COURAGE AND RISK.

—Thomas Moore

CHAPTER 14
Worth the Risk

L ook at yourself very closely to identify the mask you're wearing to impress people (or maybe in some cases, to intimidate them). Find one person with whom you can be more vulnerable than you've ever been before. Let that person see the worst in you and love you anyway, and let that person see the talents and ideas you've hidden far too long. In the safety of that relationship, share your highest hopes and biggest dreams. They may have sounded outlandish and foolish when you had less confidence, but now they begin to take on the form of a plan.

A friend of mine, Tim McNary, once told me, "I've always wanted to write a song, play the guitar, and play my music for the world."

I had known this guy for over ten years and had absolutely no idea he ever thought about music! I asked, "If that's your dream, why haven't you ever talked about it before?"

He looked a little embarrassed and told me, "Because I was afraid what people would think."

It was a huge compliment that he trusted me enough to share his dream. He continued, "But I'm too afraid to play in front of a crowd."

"How about me?"

He laughed, "I can probably do that." Next thing you know we were out on my porch and he was strumming the guitar completely in his element.

Because some really good friends have been real with me and given me confidence, I could do that for him. I was paying forward the confidence others have instilled in me. By the way, it turns out Tim McNary is a really good musician. Years later he has released several albums, moved to Nashville, and has toured across the U.S. playing shows of his original songs. Well done, Tim.

It took Tim 10 seconds of insane courage to take off his mask, be honest about his hopes, and tell me what he really wanted to do. For him and for any of the rest of us who struggle with this fear, the risk of being exposed is maybe the one thing we've avoided all our lives. It doesn't seem like it would take "insane courage" to talk honestly with a friend, but it does. I assure you it does.

When your friend imparts confidence, you'll find the courage to take off and fly. If failure isn't a blot on your identity, you can afford to take risks. And if you can learn to enjoy success without discounting it or feeling crushed under the pressure of higher expectations, you'll be willing to take more risks . . . in your career, in your most important relationships, and in every other part of your life.

UNCERTAINTY AND MYSTERY ARE

ENERGIES OF LIFE. DON'T LET THEM SCARE YOU

UNDULY, FOR THEY KEEP BOREDOM AT BAY

AND SPARK CREATIVITY.

—*R. I. Fitzhenry*

10 Seconds Starts Now
ROAD TO COURAGE

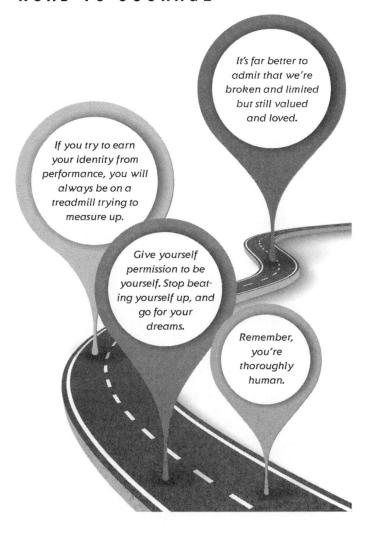

It's far better to admit that we're broken and limited but still valued and loved.

If you try to earn your identity from performance, you will always be on a treadmill trying to measure up.

Give yourself permission to be yourself. Stop beating yourself up, and go for your dreams.

Remember, you're thoroughly human.

**FEAR SAYS,
"WHO ARE YOU KIDDING? YOU'LL NEVER SUCCEED."**

**COURAGE RESPONDS,
"IF NOT YOU, THEN WHO?"**

FEAR FACTOR 4

Fear of the First Step:
Hips Don't Lie

**FEAR SAYS,
"YOU CAN ALWAYS DO IT LATER."**

**COURAGE RESPONDS,
"YOU'RE ONLY GUARANTEED TODAY."**

CHAPTER 15

Mañana, Always Mañana

"Lips Don't Lie" just doesn't sound right, does it? Luckily the song title was changed and history was forever made with "Hips Don't Lie." Everybody under, oh, 70 (and a bunch of people older than that) are ready to get up and dance when they hear those words. No matter where you are, when you hear Shakira belt out that beat, you want to get up and dance! She is a Colombian sensation and a global megastar. I'm a huge fan . . . even if my hips don't exactly move like hers!

We would never have heard of her if she hadn't taken the first step. When we look at Shakira's incredible career, we might think success has come easily for her. Could someone like her need 10 seconds of insane courage from time to time? Has she faced crucial moments when the odds were long and the obstacles daunting? It turns out that she has faced those moments several times.

At the young age of four, her father took her to a Middle Eastern restaurant. There, she heard captivating music and watched belly dancers. She got on the table and started dancing. From that moment, she was determined to be a performer. The path, however, wasn't exactly seamless. When Shakira was in the second grade, her music teacher told her she sounded "like a goat," and she was rejected by the school choir. She struggled with ADHD and was often sent out of class for being disruptive. Sometimes after school she performed belly dances for her classmates. Her behavior in school, however, wasn't a reflection of her mental acuity. She speaks five languages and has an IQ of 140. Casual.

When she was still a child, a Sony music executive held an audition for her in a hotel lobby. When he took the tape to his director, however, he wasn't impressed. The executive didn't give up. He arranged for a surprise audition, and this time, the director signed her for three albums. Her debut album was recorded when she was only 13 years old. For years, she recorded and performed in Latin America, but she was virtually unknown in the United States and Europe. She broke through in 2001 with her album *Laundry Service*, featuring another hit single, "Whenever, Wherever." Two years later, she recorded a song for the movie, *The Italian Job,* starring Charlize Theron and Mark Walberg.

The performance that I think best represents Shakira's life is the song she did for the children's movie, *Zootopia*: it's called "Try Everything." The animated movie is about a bunny who wants to become a police officer, a seemingly impossible dream. It shows the rabbit, a kudu, a hippo, a tiger, and lots of other animals being inspired by the message (and the beat) of Shakira's song. The lyrics are perfect for anyone who is afraid of taking the first step:

> I won't give up
> No, I won't give in till I reach the end
> And then I'll start again
> No, I won't leave
> I want to try everything
> I want to try even though I could fail . . .
>
> I won't give up
> No, I won't give in till I reach the end
> And then I'll start again
> No, I won't leave
> I want to try everything
> I want to try even though I could fail.[15]

I know people who are paralyzed by the fear of failure, so they avoid any risk, any first step that might lead to anything less than complete, unfiltered success. Guarantees are attractive, but they are unrealistic. Singing and dancing in front of a global audience is certainly putting it all out there (especially when one of your songs is "Hips Don't Lie"!), but all of us have dreams we want to fulfill. They may be big or small, but they're very important to us. We'll never realize them, though, if we don't act in those 10 seconds of insane courage to take the first step. If we take that one step, we may not do it perfectly, or even well, but we can make changes along the way . . . as long as we keep moving. Throughout her life, Shakira hasn't said, "Mañana"; she has said, "Hoy!"

Our first step may be about a career, a relationship, a purpose, or a way to serve others. When she was 19, Shakira started her Bare Feet Foundation, which has provided education and jobs for over 30,000 Colombians. She's just beginning. In Latin America, 54 million children are five and under, and 32 million of them live in poverty. She hasn't touched them all yet, but she's taken the first steps.

PROCRASTINATION: EVERYONE'S WORST ENEMY

Procrastination speaks to all of us, and every time we hear the voice of delay, it sounds reasonable and right. People in business say they need to see one more report before they can make a decision, they need one more marketing analysis, and they want a consensus on the team before they pull the trigger. Or they want to wait to share their best ideas until they rise to a particular position in the company.

Students believe they can cram the night before the exam, and besides, they have so many things to do that are more fun than studying. To make major decisions, they want to wait until the end of the semester, the summer break, next year, or after they get another degree.

People who are dating (at least one of the pair) have seen too much trauma in the lives of friends who have gotten married, so they insist on waiting until they're "absolutely sure," all their fears are relieved, and the future looks perfect.

Couples sometimes wait to have children until their careers are established and they have enough money in the bank to give them plenty of cushion, even if that time doesn't arrive until they're 50.

Individuals may wait to start exercising until they have the right gym membership, the right workout clothes, or they've lost enough weight so they look okay in their skin-tight clothes when they look in the mirror.

The classic problem that plagues many people is their diet. They know they need to lose a few pounds, but they claim, "I'll start tomorrow . . . or next week . . . or after this holiday . . . or sometime (ambiguous and undefined) in the future."

Whether the procrastinators are in business, college, a dating relationship, marriage, or any other season of life, each one insists, "I just want to be thorough, prepared, and ready."

Patience is a virtue, and planning is crucial for people in every line of work and every stage of life. But there's a line between common sense and fear. When we cross it, we're not being wise and prudent; we're letting our fear of making the wrong decision prevent us from moving forward.

We think we are rational, but most procrastinators live by the vague, amorphous feeling that "things just aren't right yet." They expect to have all their questions answered and all their anxieties alleviated before they take the step. That seldom, if ever, happens, so they stay stuck in an endless time warp.

I LOVE DEADLINES. I LOVE THE WHOOSHING NOISE

THEY MAKE AS THEY GO BY.

—Douglas Adams

"Reasonable" Delays

We've already looked at many of the statements we tell ourselves to justify delayed actions, but here are a few more favorites:

"There's no hurry. I'll start tomorrow."

"I'll start when the time is right."

"I'll get to it when . . ."

"Yep, that's on my Bucket List. Someday I'll get to it."

"Yep, that's one of my New Year's resolutions. I'll start then."

"I'm too old/young, too inexperienced, haven't been here long enough."

"Instead of that, I'll just keep doing this."

"What's the hurry?"

"I can't. I'm busy."

"Surely somebody will stop this madness! (I'll watch and see.)"

"I'm still not ready yet."

CHAPTER 16

This Is the Day

We know him as "The Rock," but Dwayne Johnson's career sometimes looked more like sediment washed up on the shores of failure. Again and again, he had to make the decision to take a step, a new first step, and see where it might lead.

Professional wrestling was in his blood. His grandfather was Peter "High Chief" Fanene Maivia, and his father, Rocky Johnson, was also a wrestler. Dwayne, though, took a different athletic path. He played college football at the University of Miami, known in his playing days as one of the premier programs in the nation. It seemed he was destined for the NFL, but a back injury made that impossible. He tried a team with the Canadian Football League, but he didn't make the cut.

With few career prospects, Johnson followed his father and grandfather into the ring. His first bout in the World Wrestling Federation came in Texas against the Brooklyn Brawler. Soon, the federation changed his name to Flex Kavana, but a year later, he became The Rock. He inspired love and hatred in his famous feud with Steve Austin. He won the WWF Heavyweight title six times and the Tag Team championship five times.

Johnson had it made in his chosen sport, but he decided to take another chance: acting. He sometimes played evil characters in *The Mummy Returns* and *Scorpion King*, and he played tough guys in films like *Fast & Furious*. He eventually got roles as heroes, like *Hercules* and *San Andreas*. But we've also seen his softer side in the animated movie *Moana*. The series of movie titles signify remarkable growth in his acting talents.

All of these career iterations—football, wrestling, and the morphing of movie roles—represent a series of first steps. From a distance, we may think of them as a logical and even inevitable series, but each one represents a new challenge, new risks, and new opportunities to succeed or fail.

Along the way, Johnson faced plenty of self-doubts. As he distanced himself from wrestling and embraced his acting career, he realized he didn't really fit either place any longer. In an interview for *Esquire*, he remembered the moment he had to face some hard realities:

> The big stars didn't look like me—and I didn't look like them. There wasn't a blueprint or a model. *Well, here's a former football player who once wrestled and he's this height and this weight. He's black and Samoan and he has tattoos.* . . . And then it was slim down, stop working out as much, get distance from wrestling and the moniker of the Rock. There were a lot of changes—the people around me at that time felt like it was the best thing to do, but by the way, I bought into it. I embraced it. Well, like anything, when you start being someone else, not being yourself, you may get lucky and it may work for a little while, but it's gonna come back and bite you eventually. So there was a big moment of clarity in about 2010—I just felt, Yeah, this isn't working. I need to stop, readjust, reassess, and change everything around me—and I gotta take one more shot, but at least I'm gonna take a shot with me being myself.[16]

Johnson started his own film production company. He named it Seven Bucks Production because he remembers the moment after he was cut from a Canadian Football League team. He didn't have a car, and his father had to drive from Miami to the team's training camp in Tampa to pick him up. All he had in his wallet at the time was a five and two ones: seven bucks. One of his Miami teammates had signed an NFL contract for millions, but Dwayne had only seven dollars to his name. He was angry and disappointed, but he refused to give up. He took the next first step into wrestling, then into movies as a bad guy, and then into more nuanced roles. The amazing career of Dwayne Johnson, The Rock, is a long series of first steps.

REASONS AND EXCUSES

Let's face it. People procrastinate. We want to feel in control of our lives, and procrastinating promises we can avoid risks that make us feel uncomfortable. We want guaranteed outcomes, but almost any decision carries uncertainty, so it's easier just to defer as many choices as possible.

Another reason we delay is that what we are doing now may appear to be easier than the task we're putting off. In this way, the future payoff seems less attractive, and in fact, even a loss. Psychologist Elliott T. Berkman observes that the problem is usually "a product of motivation, rather than ability. In other words, you can be really good at something, whether it's cooking a gourmet meal or writing a story, but if you don't possess the motivation, or sense of importance, to complete the task, it'll likely be put off."[17] Simply put: we can do it; we just don't value the outcome of action as much as we value the safety of inaction.

When we choose to avoid deciding and taking action, most of us don't just sit there. We find unthreatening distractions that occupy our minds and our time. As we do them, we have some sense of being busy, of accomplishing something, and we tell ourselves the tradeoff of the actual distraction compared to the potential risk is worth it. We play video games, check social media, daydream of an exciting life, sleep, watch YouTube, binge watch a show, or read books to escape.

Delays, then, seem attractive and logical . . . but this pattern numbs our souls and causes us to miss countless opportunities.

OVER THE WALL

Irish author Frank O'Connor recounted a story of his childhood when he and his friends encountered an orchard wall that seemed too high for them to climb. After careful analysis, one of them had an idea. He threw his hat over the wall, so they had no choice but to find a way to climb over it. Years later, President Kennedy told O'Connor's story in San Antonio the day before his death. He used it as a metaphor to encourage people to take bold action on one of his biggest dreams: NASA and the space program. He told the crowd, "This nation has tossed its cap over the wall of space, and we have no choice but to follow it."[18]

When we're tempted to delay too long, to wait until all the conditions are just right and we have no misgivings, it's smart to take an action that commits us to follow through.

PROCRASTINATION IS OPPORTUNITY'S ASSASSIN.

—Victor Kiam

No More Waiting

We need to remind ourselves:

"Time is my most fleeting resource."

"Procrastination is full of false promises."

"What are the real opportunities of today?"

"I need to do something today. I'll be glad I did tomorrow."

"I need to listen to the voice and do something about it."

"Life only gets more complicated with age. Do it now!"

"I can start small, but I need to start now."

"It often takes twice as long as anyone expects, so I need to start now."

"There's never "a perfect time.""

"If it keeps me up at night, it's probably what I need to do . . . right now!"

"In this moment, in this situation, what does it mean to throw my cap over the wall?"

CHAPTER 17

Jump Now

You may recall that when I came back to the University of Georgia, I intentionally didn't take enough credits to graduate. I went back overseas to Kenya, where I volunteered at the orphanage and met Martin, the little boy who changed the direction of my life.

When I arrived back home, I enrolled for the spring semester to take my last class. At the end of the semester, I applied to be the student graduation speaker. I got it, and I couldn't have been more excited. They warned me, though, that I was supposed to only be a small part in the big event. They have really important people speaking at graduation. The clear message was, "You're not one of those important people, so watch it, kid." The committee gave me a seven-minute time limit, and they required an advance copy of the speech so they could review it.

By this point in my life, my dream of starting a non-profit to help kids affected by HIV/AIDS, just like Martin, was planted in my heart and consuming all my thoughts. Speaking at graduation would be the moment to announce to all 30,000 people—graduates and their families—that I was going to take the leap. If I said it in front of all those people, I was throwing my cap over the wall . . . no turning back.

The problem was that it would take much longer than seven minutes to describe my experiences in Nairobi at the orphanage, and particularly, with Martin. I scrapped the talk I had given the committee, and I prepared the one I knew I had to give.

I got up to speak under the watchful eyes of the graduation committee and 30,000 others packed into a football stadium. I poured out my heart for 17 minutes. Oops. I painted the picture of a new organization to care for those who were largely forgotten, if not shunned, by most of the people around them. I said, "Everybody can be a hero for someone, at some time, in some place. Our time is now." I then shared my last conversation with Martin when he said, "GG, GG. You are my favorite friend in the whole world, and I know that best friends keep promises. I want you to promise you'll always remember me." I told the audience, "I promised Martin I'd always remember him. So today, I am starting H.E.R.O. for Children, a charity to improve the quality of life for children with HIV/AIDS, as one of the ways to fulfill that promise. I hope you will join me in this effort."

I decided to talk to the parents as well as the graduating students: "The actions we take will be different for each person, but I know this: When we're young, there's a voice inside all of us that says we can accomplish great things. As we get older, if we don't listen to that voice and act on it, it fades farther and farther away, until one day, it may never come back again. I was inspired by a ten-year-old boy named Martin, and I promised I'd never forget him."

I left my prepared notes and told them honestly, "I may walk so far out on that branch that it might break or I might fall off in these efforts. But I'm listening to that still, small voice inside of me, and I'm going for it. I would like to invite you to become a hero for one of these kids and step into their lives and care for them as a mentor or a role model or any way you can. We need your help to be a hero, a H.E.R.O. for Children."

At about the ten-minute mark of my speech, I'm sure the members of the committee wanted a CIA surgical drone strike to take me out, but I had the stage. By the time I sat down, my cap was way over the wall! I had no options: I had to start the nonprofit, but I wondered what the price might be for this step. There were a few minor problems: Did I have an organization to help these kids? No. Did I know any of these kids? Not here in the U.S. Did I have any medical expertise or contacts with professionals who care for kids like these? None at all. Did I have any resources to start? Zip. Nada. I had no clue how to make all this happen, but I had just invited 30,000 people to join me.

I had a pretty good idea what the committee thought of my bending of their time limit, but shockingly, I didn't hear from any of them. Instead, two of them who were in the audience that day wanted to know more about my ideas. They were Athletic Director and Hall of Fame football coach Vince Dooley and the head football coach, Mark Richt. That very next week, my co-founder Ryan Gembala and I were in Coach Richt's office and he was asking how he could help.

When we met, Coach Richt was moved by the vision of helping kids all around the state of Georgia. He said, "I can help you, but you really need Coach Dooley to get onboard. I'll make that connection for you." Coach Richt and Coach Dooley became our first board members . . . even before we had a board of directors.

As life would have it, Ryan had spent a summer in Brazil working at an orphanage as well. We had similar experiences on two different continents and decided to co-found the organization together. His dad gave us some office space, and the two of us gave every moment of every day (or so it seemed) to get this nonprofit up and running. We were paid $500 a month for over two years—so little money that both of us had to move back in with our parents—but the sense of importance was far bigger than the inconvenience or embarrassment. No excuses. No delays.

H.E.R.O. for Children became the largest pediatric HIV/AIDS organization in Georgia and then one of the largest in the Southeast focused on quality of life care. We had mentoring programs, summer camps, a Christmas program, and a college readiness program, in addition to providing a wide range of resources for the kids. Thousands of UGA students have participated as philanthropists and mentors, and millions of dollars have been raised for the cause since it began.

Ten years later, we had a gala to commemorate the anniversary of H.E.R.O. for Children. We honored Coach Dooley and Coach Richt for all they had done for the organization. The charity continues today, still making a difference in the lives of children every year.

We can find a hundred reasons to put things off. We only need one better reason to seize the moment and take action.

YOU . . . NOW . . . TODAY

I don't have to tell you it's time to take the step you've been putting off. You already know that. The problem is that delays have become a habit. It's so easy now to put it off one more time, and one more time, and one more time. Each time you wait, your heart becomes a little hardened, hope dies a little more, and you wonder if you'll ever take the step. This hope may be buried under years of fear and denial, but if you're still breathing, it's still there.

You've come to the 10 seconds when you need insane courage. The act itself may not be monumental, but taking the action changes the entrenched habit of years. You know what to do. You've imagined it thousands of times before. Maybe you need to overcome procrastination at work, or maybe it's a relationship and you've dreamed about having more than a casual conversation with that guy or that girl, but you've been scared the person wouldn't return your interest. The fears have been so big and so real they've blotted out the sun, but now you begin to believe taking action is more valuable than living in the cocoon of false safety and limited risk. Doing something may produce something good . . . maybe something great!

Live with the fact there are no guarantees. Your dream has captured your heart, but the first step may be big or small. It doesn't matter. Take it. If you need something to push you, find a way to throw your cap over the wall so you're on record with people you value. Then, there's no turning back. You don't have all the answers. You may not even know most of the questions! But throw your cap and start climbing. You'll figure it out as you go.

It's time. Throw your cap over the wall. Don't wait until it feels right, because fear has a way of making nothing good ever feel right. Jump now.

Fear says, "You can always do it later."
Courage responds, "You're only guaranteed today."

DON'T WAIT.

THE TIME WILL NEVER BE JUST RIGHT.

—*Napoleon Hill*

CHAPTER 18

No More Excuses

We don't change the perspectives and habits of a lifetime in a flash, but we *begin* to change them in a flash. The change happens as we realize we're losing far more than we're gaining by putting things off. Yes, we avoided risks, but we lost joy, the chance to succeed, real relationships, and the adventure of living. That's too high a price to pay!

We stop procrastinating when we tell ourselves, "I can make a difference"; "I have good ideas"; "I can contribute"; "I'm valuable to this venture"; "It doesn't have to be airtight before I begin." Our bold new actions, then, are an expression of a more positive identity. We aren't as threatened by the risk of failure. In fact, we see failure as a way to learn and grow.

The commitment to take action puts control back in your corner. You no longer react and hide. You think, plan, and act . . . like a real person, a healthy person, a secure and confident person. Instead of trying to fade into the woodwork in the office or at home, you bet on yourself to effect real and productive change. Oh, the fears and doubts will still be there, but they no longer stop you.

We're not promised tomorrow. We have today, and we have every opportunity to make today something special. All of us hear that voice that's calling us to be something good and do something significant—large or small, organizational or interpersonal. We get to decide how long we take to respond to the voice that's calling out to us.

We don't have to have all the answers before we start. In fact, we never have all the answers at the beginning. The quicker we answer what we hear, no matter how faint or uncertain, the sooner we figure out the next steps.

GET STARTED . . . RIGHT NOW

Throw your cap. Pay for six months of guitar lessons, not just one. Pay for an annual membership at the gym. Write the proposal today so you can present it to your boss tomorrow. Ask your boss for thirty minutes of his or her time, and make sure it's on the calendar. Make the call to that girl or guy. Buy the ring and arrange a moment neither of you will ever forget. Call your dad and tell him you want to talk. Set your alarm twenty minutes earlier.

The endless delays have been a way of thinking and a way of living. The countless decisions to put things off were the natural responses to that mindset and habit. Now, fill your mind with two powerful concepts: images of the *painful consequences* of failing to follow through . . . and a vision of the *positive results* that may happen each time you have 10 seconds of insane courage to jump. You'll soon find the real benefits of developing the habit of movement far outweigh the perceived benefits of avoiding it.

Each time you find the courage to take action, recognize it and reward yourself. You deserve it. You're becoming a courageous, competent, diligent, responsible person who gets things done.

Start today. Throw your cap over the wall.

TIME IS AN EQUAL OPPORTUNITY EMPLOYER.

EACH HUMAN BEING HAS EXACTLY THE SAME

NUMBER OF HOURS AND MINUTES EVERY DAY.

RICH PEOPLE CAN'T BUY MORE HOURS.

SCIENTISTS CAN'T INVENT NEW MINUTES.

AND YOU CAN'T SAVE TIME TO SPEND IT ON

ANOTHER DAY. EVEN SO, TIME IS AMAZINGLY FAIR

AND FORGIVING. NO MATTER HOW MUCH TIME YOU'VE

WASTED IN THE PAST, YOU STILL HAVE

AN ENTIRE TOMORROW.

—*Denis Waitley*

10 Seconds Starts Now
ROAD TO COURAGE

Fill your mind with the painful consequences of not acting. Now fill your mind with the positive results that may happen when you choose courage over comfort.

Each time you wait, your heart becomes a little hardened, hope dies a little bit more, and you wonder if you'll ever take the step. Take the step.

You will never have all your questions answered and all your anxieties alleviated before you take the first step.

Try everything.

**FEAR SAYS,
"YOU CAN ALWAYS DO IT LATER."**

**COURAGE RESPONDS,
"YOU'RE ONLY GUARANTEED TODAY."**

FEAR FACTOR 5

Fear of Bailing Out: *I'm No Navy Seal!*

**FEAR SAYS,
"DON'T START. YOU'LL QUIT ANYWAY."**

**COURAGE RESPONDS,
"KEEP GOING. YOUR DREAM IS TOO GREAT
TO GIVE UP ON IT!"**

CHAPTER 19

Never Wavering

S
ome people have a dream, but they don't have tenacity, so they rarely get close to realizing their potential. They rely on luck or connections or their past success, but these only get us to the door of opportunity. They don't break the door down.

Gary Vaynerchuk has a very different idea of what people need in order to succeed. He may be crass, and he may say things that shock your mother, but his "in your face" approach is necessary to get a lot of us out of our passive daydream and onto the battlefield.

Gary was one of the first people to sell wine on the Internet, and for 18 long months no one really cared. He posted a show about wine every single day, and his small following loved it. He didn't care how long it took for his business model to catch on. He was in it for the long haul.

When he was in his 20s, he "worked his face off." In an interview, he explained that he worked six days a week: "I got to Wine Library at 7:30 in the morning and I left at 7, 8, or 9. I just worked. I just built a management staff, I tasted wine, I built up the website. Learned how to do Google AdWords. I just worked."

A few years later, his hard work paid off. His wine business had an annual revenue of $60 million, he established a media company generating over $100 million in revenue, and he wrote a best-seller, *Crush It!*[19] But that's not all. Gary formed a publishing company, became a partner in an agency representing professional athletes, and shares his ideas on his daily vlog, #DailyVee.

He hosts a show answering questions about leadership, starting businesses, digital media, wine, and anything else related to
building businesses.

In *Crush It!* he pushes people to be more and do more, to
go past their self-imposed limits: "Live your passion. What does
that mean, anyway? It means that when you get up for work every
morning, every single morning, you are pumped because you get
to talk about or work with or do the thing that interests you the
most in the world. You don't live for vacations because you don't
need a break from what you're doing—working, playing, and re-
laxing are one and the same. You don't even pay attention to how
many hours you're working because to you, it's not really work.
You're making money, but you'd do whatever it is you're doing
for free."[20]

On his vlog, he gives a ton of important advice, including: "I
put zero weight into anyone's opinion about me because I know
exactly who I am. Can you say the same? When? Don't be afraid
to break things. Don't take the time to breathe. Don't aim for perfect. And whatever you do, keep moving."[21]

To Gary, it's never time to sit back and coast. He tells people
to continually shape their message and constantly communicate
it. In his book, *Jab, Jab, Jab, Right Hook: How to Tell Your Story in a
Noisy World*, he writes, "Whether you're an entrepreneur, a small
business, or a Fortune 500 company, great marketing is all about
telling your story in such a way that it compels people to buy what
you are selling. That's a constant. What's always in flux, especially
in this noisy, mobile world, is how, when, and where the story
gets told, and even who gets to tell all of it."[22]

His business philosophy isn't complicated; it's simple and
powerful. On his vlog, he explains, "If you religiously follow just
the few core business philosophies that mean the most to you,
and spend all your time there, everything else will naturally fall
into place." And he concludes, "Life shrinks and expands on the
proportion of your willingness to take risks and try new things."

A dream has to be so big it keeps you up at night, but the fulfillment doesn't happen by magic. It takes plenty of hard work, and it requires us to bounce back after each failure. Vaynerchuk's ultimate dream is to someday buy the New York Jets football franchise. When his family immigrated to America, he was just a kid, but he fell in love with the Jets. His parents couldn't afford to buy an official team jersey, but his mother made him one. Gary wore it everywhere. He's determined to document his entire life and business story online until he has enough money to buy the Jets. He's not there yet, but who would bet against him? I once met Gary in Atlanta, and he's an amazing guy. I know he'll do it.

Do you ever start something, hit snags, and feel like quitting? Sure. All of us do (maybe except for Gary Vaynerchuk). Be ruthlessly honest about the fears welling up inside, and face them with 10 seconds of insane courage.

An article in *Forbes* magazine quantified our entrepreneurial fears: 90 percent of startup companies fail.[23] Each owner thought they were in the 10 percent. The founders may have planned for years, and many sank every dollar they had in the venture. The discouraging number of failures, though, isn't just a statistic. It doesn't take much imagination to put ourselves in their places in the months between the birth and death of their companies. We can easily identify several reasons for these failures:

- They stayed up nights and on weekends to design the very best product. They were sure it would be perfect for the market, and people would eat it up. They didn't.

- Some entrepreneurs simply aren't good at the details— the numbers and processes—necessary to run a new business. They assume their brilliance or their product will somehow overcome their lack of attention to details. It didn't.

- Sometimes the person who starts a business has asked friends to work with him or her, but friendship isn't the primary qualification for key positions. Lack of experience in important roles . . . to say nothing of gross incompetence . . . can ruin a new company's prospects. Truth.

- Many new companies fail because they are undercapitalized. The founder may have assumed sales would bring in revenues much faster than actually happened, or the timeline for production, marketing, sales, and receipts wasn't realistic. When their financials weren't solid, they weren't able to raise more capital. End of story.

- A few startups fail because they grew too fast, outpacing their capacity for production and ruining their reputation with new customers. The downside of growth.

Startups don't fail in an instant. Usually, hopes fade gradually. Doubts replace optimism, and sleepless enthusiasm turns into sleepless worry. In those long, dark nights and anxiety-filled days, people begin to waver. They wonder, *When is it time to close this down? When should I send out my résumé? When is it time to even have these conversations?*

Haunting questions, at least in the mind of the founder and the people funding the new company, are: *What if we quit one day too soon? What if we hang on one more month, one more week, or one more day to see if this will turn around? What if we can find another source of funding, another market, a better product?*

This isn't the problem of procrastination; it's the problem of persistence. People under stress are tempted to waver. It's human nature. Questions we never dreamed we'd ask are suddenly tattooed on our foreheads. Fears we never knew existed stagger us. We start looking for a way out, but we feel terribly guilty, especially if others appear to have more confidence than we can muster that it all might work out. But then, we think they're crazy.

YOU MAY ENCOUNTER MANY DEFEATS, BUT YOU MUST

NOT BE DEFEATED. IN FACT, IT MAY BE NECESSARY

TO ENCOUNTER THE DEFEATS, SO YOU CAN KNOW

WHO YOU ARE, WHAT YOU CAN RISE FROM,

HOW YOU CAN STILL COME OUT OF IT.

— *Maya Angelou*

Second Thoughts

When we waver, we may think . . .

"I may not be cut out for this."

"This is a lot harder than I thought!"

"I may never have the breakthrough moment."

"What if I start and can't finish?"

"I look at all the others who have wrecked.
Am I any different?"

"My dreams are probably too big anyway."

"What was I thinking when I started? Was I insane?"

"I need to be more reasonable."

"When is the right time to pull the plug? Is it now?
Am I already too late?"

"If I can't finish, I'll look like a fool."

CHAPTER 20

Never Say Never

We may have many different reasons why we want to bail out. The task may seem too hard, we don't feel qualified, or we don't want to fail. Perhaps even more often, we don't want to admit we *have already* failed. We bail out by shifting the blame to others, or we deny anything bad happened at all. Taking responsibility can be one of the hardest things we can do, but it's essential if we want to have even an ounce of self-respect and win the respect of the people around us.

Jocko Willink led a Navy Seal team in Ramadi during the height of the fight against the insurgency in Iraq. The house-to-house combat was fierce and confusing; the fog of war wasn't just a concept. At one point, his team, along with Army soldiers, Marines, and Iraqi allied forces, came under fire. After several minutes of a deafening firefight, they realized they were firing at friendly forces. One Iraqi lay dead, two others were wounded, and one of his Seals had been shot in the face. Friendly fire is an unspeakable tragedy. It is "the mortal sin of combat and the most horrific part of war."

When Willink got back to his base, he received a message that he and his team were under investigation. He was ordered to shut down all operations and prepare his report about the incident. As he wrote, he struggled to identify what had gone so tragically wrong. Willink knew what the investigation would find: Someone had to pay for the mistake. Someone had to be held accountable.

Willink wrote a detailed report about the failures of planning and execution of the mission. He identified who on his team or with the Army or Marines had made mistakes. There was plenty of blame to pass around, but as he identified the people responsible for each error, something didn't seem right. Only minutes before he and his team met with the commanding officer and the investigative panel, he realized the answer to his dilemma. Ultimately, there was only one person to blame for the friendly fire, the dead Iraqi, and the three who were wounded.

When the men assembled in the room with the commanding officer and the investigators, he asked his men, "What went wrong? Who is responsible for what happened? Whose fault was this?"

A SEAL raised his hand and said, "It was my fault. I didn't keep control of the Iraqi soldiers with me. They left their designated sector, and that was the root of all these problems."

Willink told him, "No, it wasn't your fault."

Another SEAL spoke up, "It was my fault. I didn't pass our location over the radio fast enough, so no one knew what building we were in. That's what caused all the confusion."

Willink replied, "No, it wasn't your fault either."

A third SEAL said, "Boss, it's my fault. I didn't properly identify my target, and I shot and killed the friendly Iraqi soldier."

Willink shook his head, "It wasn't your fault either." He then looked around the room and said, "And it wasn't yours or yours or yours or yours. There is only one person at fault, only one person to blame. That person is me. I am the commander, the senior man on the battlefield, and I am responsible for everything that happens."

At that point in the debrief, he told his commanding officer and his men about policies and procedures he was implementing that would ensure this mistake would never happen again.

Later, as he reflected on this pivotal moment in his life, he explained, "It hurt. It hurt my ego and my pride to take the blame, but I knew that to maintain my integrity as a leader and a man, I had to take responsibility. I had to control my ego so my ego didn't control me."

Willink didn't get fired. When he took ownership, without finger-pointing and blaming others, his commanding officer trusted him even more. Also, his men were convinced he would never shirk responsibility, so they trusted him even more. The men on the team followed Willink's example. His willingness to accept ownership of problems galvanized the team and made it even more effective. He remarks, "When a team takes ownership of its problems, the problems get solved. It is true on the battlefield, it is true in business, and it is true in life." He advises us, "Take extreme ownership. Don't make excuses. Don't blame any other person or thing. Get control of your ego. Don't hide your delicate pride from the truth. Take ownership of everything in your life: the bad and the good. Take ownership of your problems, and take ownership of the solutions. Take ownership of your life."[24]

IS THE DREAM WORTH IT?

All of us face obstacles as we pursue our dreams. In fact, if you don't encounter roadblocks and criticism, your dream is probably not grand enough. Don't lower the bar to avoid problems. Press through them, go over them, find a new way around them. Do whatever it takes to succeed, but don't quit. Yes, you may need to step back and regroup, but that's not quitting. You may need to get some assistance or advice, but that's not giving up. You're still looking for a path forward.

What does it take for us to give up? What makes us throw up our hands and bail out? Many leaders will tell you that their greatest success only came when they experienced "the death of their dream"—not a bump in the road but a complete disaster. When they faced it with courage and hope, they saw Phoenix rise from the ashes and a new day dawn. The resurrection of their dreams didn't happen immediately, but the process of reevaluating and retooling sharpened their vision of what could be.

You've got to want it. You have to be willing to keep going when the critics on the sidelines bark at you and your best friends think you've lost your mind, when your financials look bleak and when your competitor gets the big sale.

Persistence. It's a necessary character quality for all of us.

LET PERSEVERANCE BE YOUR ENGINE

AND HOPE YOUR FUEL.

—H. Jackson Brown, Jr.

Staying In

When we're tempted to waver, we need to tell ourselves . . .

"The only thing standing in my way are my insecurities and excuses."

"Yeah, it'll be hard, but I can do it."

"I'm stronger than anyone can imagine."

"I'll hit plenty of roadblocks, but I'll find a way over or around them."

"Even if no one believes in me, I believe in myself."

"I'll find a way."

"Perseverance produces character and character produces hope" (Romans 5:4).

"Every human has enough grit. It's a choice."

"All I need is perseverance over time."

"Pain and struggle are a sign of growth, not weakness."

"The death of a dream is the perfect time for a resurrection."

CHAPTER 21

Tenacity to Jump

T he road to 196. Since I was a kid, this was my dream: visiting all 196 countries around the world. Only a handful of humans have ever done it. Most of them are no longer alive, but those who have done it have some of the most amazing stories I've ever heard. I've had a chance to meet one of them.

But I have a lot of questions: Could I really do it? *Should* I really do it? Do I have the tenacity to actually do it? I've had a lot of crazy dreams in my life, but truth be told, this is the one that has always jumped out whenever I think about where I want my life to go. Let me explain how this dream got started.

When I was eight years old, my Mom (the notorious "Fran G" to all my friends) gave me two things for Christmas: a globe and a huge, 26-volume encyclopedia set. Thanks, Mom. What were you thinking? As I recall, she blamed Santa for that debacle. These are not the types of gifts that elicit excitement on Christmas morning when you're in elementary school, but actually, my Mom knew what she was doing. After I got over my initial disappointment, the two presents created countless hours of intrigue. I remember spinning the globe time and again wondering where my finger would land. Wherever it stopped, I looked up the country in the encyclopedia and read all about it. (I promise I also had a normal childhood . . . sort of.)

Our family never had the money to travel outside the United States. A lack of resources, though, didn't stop my Mom from dreaming big dreams for my brother Jeff and me. She always encouraged us to read about all the countries of the world, and she planted the hope to actually go to those places described in the encyclopedia. I believed her. Was this her secret and incredibly effective parenting technique to get a kid to read and dream big? Who knows, but it worked.

As you might guess, I was a bit of a rambunctious child, often the class clown and always getting myself and others into trouble. In middle school, I had quite the reputation for creating havoc during spelling tests. Finally, my beleaguered teacher had had enough. She demanded a meeting with my mother. I was a good student, but that was part of the problem. I finished tests far too early and created chaos while the other students were still working. Enter the road to 196.

My Mom and my teacher hatched a plan, one that had far bigger benefits than they ever imagined. My teacher agreed to give me one "extra credit point" on the test for every country and capital I could write down. I spent an entire year trying to ace a test and get 196 points of extra credit. I memorized all the countries and capitals of the world. During tests, I wrote frantically to get all of them on paper before time expired. I learned a lot, and I was completely occupied for the entire test period. No antics, no chaos, no disruption of the class. It was a win-win.

As I got older, I never gave up on the dream of visiting every country in the world. When I turned 30, I decided to give myself a decade to accomplish the seemingly impossible. It all started with taking my tuxedo down to Antarctica to have my picture taken on the ice and look like the penguins. If I could knock off the frozen continent and kiss a penguin for good luck, I figured I would be well on my way. Luckily, I survived. In the past few years, I've stepped foot, legally, in Cuba, North Korea (yes, North), Myanmar, and even alongside the statues of Easter Island.

The road was filled with ridiculous adventures in these turbulent countries, but also, incredible memories I'll never forget.

In Havana, Cuba, I remember getting pulled on stage at a restaurant and winning a salsa dance contest by adding a bit of hip hop to the elegance of salsa. Part disaster, part winning formula—100 percent of my Atlanta roots coming through in the Caribbean nation. The locals laughed the entire time and named me the winner. In North Korea, an embassy official told me that anything we said or did would be monitored and recorded during our time in the "Hermit Kingdom." This included our free time at a bowling alley and bonfire on the beach. Who knew either of those existed in the most terrifying country in the world?

But my favorite memories of my travels are the interesting people that stretch my imagination, like my friend Stuart Cook. He's a massive Australian rugby player whom I met in New Delhi, India and who later hosted me in Bangkok, Thailand. He was a CEO helping bring fast, casual Mexican food to Asia, and he also gave away one million burritos to those in need through a "get one-give one" campaign. And if that wasn't crazy enough, he took off a year to do an around-the-world honeymoon with his wife Samantha. As I talked with him, my mind exploded thinking of how any of his story might relate to me, or how any of that was even possible . . . but I loved it.

I have fond memories of my 100-day journey across Africa from Kenya to Cape Town. During my time in Rwanda, I was trekking with silverback gorillas in the wild, but I also heard first-hand accounts of the genocide that took the lives of over a million Rwandans. That journey led me to speak at a leadership conference in Nairobi alongside the President of Kenya and later I lived off a dollar a day with students in a township in South Africa. Each country has opened my eyes to a world made up of unique and fascinating people that drive me to see more, be more, and do more.

But at some point, you wonder whether to keep going, or if it's time to "grow up." Society has a way of diminishing your dreams when they're, well, beyond normal. How long should you hold on to a dream, regardless of how outlandish it may be? I wrestle with this question, but I've been inspired to come up with an answer. I love the movie *Yes Man* with Jim Carey. It's a comedy about a man who is compelled to say "yes" to every question and every offer. In the next season in life, I would love to go for it and say "yes" to finishing the goal of 196. I've been to 86 so far, so 110 more seems a long way off. I have no idea how I'm going to get there, but I'm not giving up. In fact, I'm not even slowing down! Who knows how I'll get to them all, but I'm certainly going to try. I can envision myself in desperately remote locations, working on my laptop while learning about fascinating places that were once childhood dreams staring back at me from the pages of an encyclopedia.

Some of us are afraid to dream because we don't want the pain of disappointment. It's safer, we conclude, to avoid even trying. Here's my advice: Get over it. You may have an impossible dream about starting a company, reinventing your career, finding the right relationship, running a marathon, or any of a million other high hopes and great goals. Don't ignore those dreams, and don't give up on them. See the possibilities as much as you see the obstacles, and keep moving forward.

When the opportunity presents itself, will you say "yes" and keep going? Will you refuse to stop even when it's difficult, or you're getting older, or it doesn't fit with a career plan, or people think you're nuts? Or will you say "yes" because it's different, courageous, and inspiring?

Here's the other thing: If you say "yes" to your highest, most inspiring dreams, you'll almost certainly have a powerful and positive impact on at least a few others who are watching you. I'm not talking about the ones who are cynical. I'm talking about the people whose dreams have a fuse and need only a spark to light it. Your courage will help them overcome their fears and do something great.

So . . . why not? For yourself and for those who are watching, go for it. Take the first step and see where it takes you. It only takes 10 seconds of insane courage.

Fear says, "Don't start. You'll quit anyway."
Courage responds, "Keep going. Your dream is too great
to give up on!"

**MEN WANTED FOR HAZARDOUS JOURNEY. LOW
WAGES, BITTER COLD, LONG HOURS OF COMPLETE
DARKNESS. SAFE RETURN DOUBTFUL. HONOUR AND
RECOGNITION IN EVENT OF SUCCESS.**

*—Recruiting ad for men to join Ernest
Shackleton on a journey to Antarctica, 1914*

CHAPTER 22

Grit

Angela Duckworth started life with a deficit: her father was a gifted scientist who wasn't impressed with her intellectual acuity. He often reminded her that she lacked any hint of genius. Her father's negative evaluation could have crushed Angela, but instead it drove her. She completed a degree in neurobiology at Harvard, received a master's in neuroscience at Oxford, and earned a Ph.D. in psychology at the University of Pennsylvania.

In her studies and professional life, she did research on cadets at West Point, teachers in struggling school districts, and finalists in the National Spelling Bee. She developed the theory that success isn't the product of genius, but of a powerful blend of passion and perseverance. She described her research and her conclusions in her book, *Grit*. She writes, "My own experience . . . suggests that grit grows as we figure out our life philosophy, learn to dust ourselves off after rejection and disappointment, and learn to tell the difference between low-level goals that should be abandoned quickly and higher-level goals that demand more tenacity. The maturation story is that we develop the capacity for long-term passion and perseverance as we get older."[25]

I experienced what Duckworth is describing when I started the nonprofit to help kids affected by HIV/AIDS. My passion was so intense that I was willing to break down walls to take the next steps. But passion was only half of the equation. We had to live with incredibly low pay, and we had to scrounge for resources every day to do what we wanted to do. But the money never mattered, and we didn't care how many hours it took. We were willing to do whatever it took to make it happen. I was never embarrassed to ask donors for money because I was so sure it was for the best possible cause.

When do you need a lion's share of grit? What do you do . . .

- When you're a single mom and you want to get a degree to provide more fully for your children.

- When your teenagers are drifting away from you.

- When you don't get the promotion.

- When the funding doesn't come.

- When your skills and experience don't quite fit your current role.

- When your boss doesn't understand you.

- When your spouse doesn't understand you.

- When your kids are driving you crazy.

- When the class is really hard.

- When your company hits a downturn and everyone starts pointing fingers.

- When it's your company and you hit bumps in funding or sales.

- When working out to get in shape has become grueling instead of fun.

- When you're in the middle of a 10K and it feels like your legs are on fire.

- When you visit your boyfriend or girlfriend's parents and a dark future suddenly appears.

- When you're having a hard time losing the last five pounds.

- When your best friend seems to drift away.

The list is endless because we're complex people living in a world of opportunities and stress. The point I'm trying to make is that it's absolutely crucial to have a clear and compelling reason to get up every morning. Your passion may not be your work. Instead, it may be your art or music, or you may dream about a company you want to form on your own time, but don't stop until something captures your heart and you can't get it out of your mind. Then act, and keep acting. Press on through the difficulties. See them as stepping stones instead of roadblocks. They won't kill you if you won't let them. Keep learning. Never quit. Be known as someone who never gives up on your dream.

OVER TIME, GRIT IS WHAT SEPARATES FRUITFUL LIVES FROM AIMLESSNESS.

—*John Ortberg*

10 Seconds Starts Now
ROAD TO COURAGE

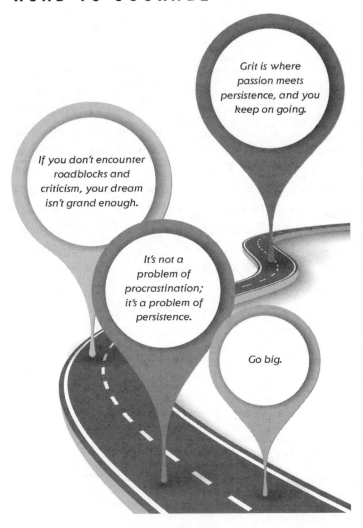

FEAR SAYS,
"DON'T START. YOU'LL QUIT ANYWAY."

COURAGE RESPONDS,
"KEEP GOING. YOUR DREAM IS TOO GREAT TO GIVE UP ON IT!"

FEAR FACTOR 6

Fear of Not Having Enough:
What Gatsby Never Knew

**FEAR SAYS,
"YOU DON'T HAVE THE RESOURCES TO BE SUCCESSFUL."**

**COURAGE RESPONDS,
"YOUR RESOURCEFULNESS IS WORTH MORE
THAN ANY RESOURCES."**

CHAPTER 23

Never Enough

F Scott Fitzgerald's *Great Gatsby* is a story of a man who had it all but never had enough. Jay Gatsby met Daisy Buchanan briefly during World War I, but he never forgot her. After the war, he lives a lavish lifestyle on Long Island, and he throws parties that are the envy of everyone in the area. When he discovers a neighbor actually knows Daisy, he asks him to arrange an introduction . . . a reintroduction. The problem is that she is now married.

Gatsby and Daisy begin a torrid affair. When her husband Tom finds out, he's furious, even though he's involved in his own affairs. At a hotel in New York, Tom confronts Gatsby and tells Daisy that Gatsby's fortune has come from bootlegging liquor during Prohibition. He's a fraud . . . a very rich fraud.

On his way back to Long Island, Gatsby's car hits Tom's mistress and kills her. But actually, Daisy had been the driver. The mistress's husband discovers it was Gatsby's car that killed his wife. Spoiler Alert: he travels to the mansion on Long Island where he shoots Gatsby before killing himself.

The web of lies, contempt, manipulation, heartache, and murder can all be traced back to Jay Gatsby's fabulous wealth and empty heart. He didn't want what he had, but he desperately wanted what he didn't have. Gatsby never found the source of real happiness and fulfillment. And it killed him.

A friend of mine, Josh Plemmons, wrote a blog called "The Financial Wisdom of Rap Music." It's hilarious and worth the read at ExtraGuacBlog.com. Within the post, he quotes the lyrics of 2 Chainz. Simply put, it's never enough: relationships, power . . . and especially, money. The three stanzas end with a crescendo of wanting more, always more: "I want me a milli," "I want me a bil-li," "I want me a trilli." After each one, he concludes, "I'm gettin' it, I'm gettin' it, no really I'm gettin' it."[26]

There's something deep in the human psyche that drives us (but not all of us in the same way) to never be satisfied with what we have. Whether it's the richest person on the planet or those who are scraping to get by, we *want* more . . . we *expect* more . . . we *demand* more. When we get a bump in salary, bonus, rec-ognition, or anything else, it feels so good, but only for a short while. Soon, the insatiable thirst for more makes us feel empty and thirsty again.

Our wants aren't optional. They're deeply embedded in the soul of every person. The challenge is to connect our deepest desires to things that really matter. In his Kenyon College com-mencement speech, author David Foster Wallace explained that our deepest longing is actually a form of worship—a transcen-dent longing. If our minds and hearts are focused on transient things, even our best efforts leave us empty and confused. He told the students and their families:

> If you worship money and things, if they are where you tap real meaning in life, then you will never have enough, never feel you have enough. It's the truth. Worship your body and beauty and sexual allure and you will always feel ugly. And when time and age start showing, you will die a million deaths before they finally grieve you. . . . Worship power, you will end up feeling weak and afraid, and you will need ever more power over others to numb you to your own fear. Worship your intellect, being seen as smart, you will end up feeling stupid, a fraud, always

on the verge of being found out. But the insidious thing about these forms of worship is not that they're evil or sinful, it's that they're unconscious. They are default settings.[27]

To Wallace, worship isn't something some people do for an hour on Sundays. It's what our hearts delight in, what our minds are fixed on, and what our dreams tell us is our real treasure. We may say we value honesty, truth, and love, but we need to look carefully at our thoughts and desires, and especially our anxieties and fears, to identify what is truly most important to us.

I WAS WITHIN AND WITHOUT,

SIMULTANEOUSLY ENCHANTED AND REPELLED

BY THE INEXHAUSTIBLE VARIETY OF LIFE.

—Gatsby

Wanting More

When we long for more and can't be satisfied, we try to tell ourselves:

"If I can just have a little more money . . ."

"If I can just have a little more prestige . . ."

"If I can just wear nicer clothes . . ."

"If I can just impress people a little more with my intelligence . . ."

"If I can just have the right shape or build . . ."

"I'll be satisfied when . . ."

"I'll have plenty when I have . . ."

"I need all the money up front if I'm going to start."

"It's got to be better than this. No one would ever invest in this the way it is."

"Money is the greatest resource."

"Popularity is the greatest thrill."

"I'll have enough when I have as much as _____."

"Having plenty of money guarantees peace of mind."

"Comparison? Sure, everybody does it."

"Competition? It's my way of life."

CHAPTER 24

Resourcefulness, Not Resources

Somewhere along the way, it dawned on me that my attention needed to shift from being focused on how many *resources* I had in my hand to how much *resourcefulness* I could employ. One is energized by comparison and competition; the other is propelled by creativity and hope. The words sound a lot alike, but the effects are worlds apart.

When we look at the amount of resources we have in our hands, we may become disappointed . . . and resentful of those who have more. We always have more resourcefulness, if we'll only realize our potential. When we compare our money, power, or talent with others', we'll always find people who have more than we have. Too often, it's a no-win game.

Comparison can inspire us to be better and do better, but if we're not careful, it will poison us with envy (someone has something that we're sure rightfully belongs to us) or jealousy (we're afraid someone will take away something or someone belonging to us).

Comparison operates in a narrow sphere. Lawyers aren't envious of artists or scientists. They're bothered by the applause other lawyers receive and the amount of money they win. Scientists envy scientists, lawyers envy lawyers, artists envy artists, and techies envy techies. This envy drives us to compete instead of caring for each other. In his classic work, *Mere Christianity*, C. S. Lewis observed that the root of envy is pride-fueled comparison:

> Pride gets no pleasure out of having something, only out of having more of it than the next man. We say that people are proud of being rich, or clever, or good-looking, but they are not. They are proud of being richer, or cleverer, or better-looking than others. If everyone else became equally rich, or clever, or good-looking there would be nothing to be proud about. It is the comparison that makes you proud; the pleasure of being above the rest. Once the element of competition is gone, pride has gone. That is why I say that Pride is essentially competitive in a way the other vices are not.[28]

When you work for a company, just getting a paycheck is immensely satisfying for a while. Then you realize a lot of others in the company are making more than you, so you begin jockeying for the next position up . . . and the next . . . and the next. You smile as you work with people each day, but you live with an undercurrent of dissatisfaction . . . suspicion of anyone who might not contribute to your next promotion . . . and resentment of those who have gotten in your way.

Or you start a business, and you're ecstatic when you have enough orders or clients to pay the bills. You can finally relax, but then, wouldn't it be great to have a bigger order or another client. Yeah, that's more like it! And then more and more: a milli, a billi, a trilli. Satisfaction comes in brief spurts, but it's soon replaced with the familiar groaning of "more," "bigger," "faster," "richer."

Some of us aren't focused on money and power. Our longing is for comfort and pleasure. Our thoughts drift to having the latest technology, a nicer apartment or home, or more vacation time. When we get those, we feel great . . . but only for a while.

Living on a rollercoaster is a lifelong habit for most of us. The carrot at the end of the stick—whether it's comfort, pleasure, power, control, prestige, or possessions—promises joy, peace, and love, but it can't deliver, at least for very long. Like a ride, there are very high highs that feel so right, but they're always followed by lows of emptiness, sadness, and loneliness.

We need to shift our focus from our resources to our resourcefulness—all the latent talent, ingenuity, and intelligence God has given us. It's time to use it!

LIFE'S TOO SHORT TO HANG OUT WITH PEOPLE WHO AREN'T RESOURCEFUL.

—Jeff Bezos

More, Really More

We often assume our options are limited by our resources, but creative (and maybe even desperate) resourcefulness opens new doors. When we feel limited, we need bigger, brighter, bolder thoughts:

"Resourcefulness is my greatest resource."

"The barter system is alive and well. I'll find a way to get what I need."

"Great ideas often start in garages."

"Live on less: give and invest."

"Never quit. Find a different door."

"There's always one more option to consider."

"I won't stop dreaming, imagining, and looking for ways I never thought about to get the job done."

CHAPTER 25

Jump In

After transitioning to the Board of H.E.R.O. for Children, I helped co-found a study abroad company called Global L.E.A.D. With a focus on Leadership, Education, Adventure, and Diplomacy, we wanted to create a social impact study-abroad program with an edge. When we wanted to launch the company, we needed to raise enough money for our team to take a 100-day trek across Africa to scout locations for the study abroad program. This wasn't going to be a joyride. We had to do the grunt work to find local organizations to partner with us, identify specific locations, check security, get permissions from local authorities, and secure housing for the students who would come.

The four people on our team—Robbie Reese, Courtney Doran, Kevin Scott, and I—planned to travel from Nairobi, Kenya to Cape Town, South Africa, and stop in a number of other cities along the way. It was a reconnaissance mission. We soon realized the logistics of setting up this kind of program were far more extensive than anything we'd done before—and for the sake of our students and their parents, we couldn't afford to screw it up.

When we ran the numbers, we estimated we would need $100,000 for the trip, the permissions, and everything else to get us up and running for the first year. We asked family and friends for money. We got a little. We sent out letters to a wider group of friends and acquaintances, but we didn't get much more. Our fundraising strategy wasn't working, and our departure date was fast approaching.

We knew some wealthy people in Atlanta, and we were sure that if we had the opportunity to talk to them face to face, they'd write big checks and we'd be on our way. We sent out invitations and held a fundraising event. We were cutting it close . . . really close. It was only two days before our flight left. About 100 of the most successful people we knew showed up, and they listened intently to our vision and our request for donations. I was sure we'd raise all the money in an instant. In fact, I wondered what we'd do with the extra we'd receive.

The gathering was everything we could have hoped, except for one thing: We raised less than a third of what we needed.

I was really surprised and deeply discouraged. We'd done the best things we knew to do to raise money. We had exhausted our best ideas, and we had exhausted our resources. We were short $70,000 with two days to go. The other three looked at me like, "Okay, Garrett, what are we going to do now?" I had no idea. We had already used our credit cards to book flights, trains, buses, and hotels to go to the cities where we hoped to set up our programs, but we didn't have the money to pay for it all. We had set up meetings with charities across Africa. Now, we were faced with cancelling the whole thing. It wasn't like we were a little short and could cut a few corners and be okay. We weren't even close. I wondered if we needed to quit.

The four of us created a vision board and brainstormed new ideas. Nothing. We were dead in the water. Doomed. Then I had one more idea, a "Hail Mary" option if there ever was one.

A few years earlier when we started H.E.R.O. for Children, I met a man named Jesse Peel, who worked with the Elton John AIDS foundation. In the early days of H.E.R.O. for Children, we applied for a grant from the foundation, and he interviewed us. In the middle of our presentation, Jesse burst out laughing because we used a PowerPoint instead of the written grant application to share our reasoning. He thought I was funny (maybe ridiculous is a better word), but he was moved by my story about Martin.

When I finished, he said, "I think your heart's in the right place, and you're going to do some great work through your organization." I may not have impressed him with our presentation to get the grant, but he liked what we were doing and believed in our mission.

Jesse and I had stayed in touch through the years and became great friends along the way. He became a donor, supporter, and meaningful advocate for our organization. At this moment for our new study abroad company, he was our best hope. Actually, he was our only hope.

I told Robbie, Courtney, and Kevin, "Well, I know a grand total of one guy who might help us at this point. His name is Jesse Peel. I'm pretty sure he has the money, but I have no idea if he's willing to invest it in us. I'm not going to ask him to give us the money. I'm going to ask him for a personal loan of $70,000. I don't know how I'll ever pay him back, but I'll find a way. He'll have to write a check or wire the money by tomorrow. It's our only shot."

I called Jesse and asked if we could have dinner that night. He said he was available, so we at least cleared the first hurdle. When we sat down together, I told him the plan and the story of how we got to this point. I said bluntly, "Jesse, we're out of resources and out of time. We want to reimagine study abroad and give thousands of college students the opportunity to have an experience just like I did with Martin. It was life changing for me. It'll be life changing for them."

I told Jesse about our team and our vision, and I explained that our fundraising efforts had fallen $70,000 short. I swallowed hard and said, "Jesse, you're the only person I know who might lend us this money. I completely understand if you can't or don't want to. But there are two things I know: first, you can help me fulfill my promise to Martin so I can go back to visit him as the first stop on our journey and help us create a brand new program to create these same opportunities abroad." I reminded Jesse about Martin's story and how my promise to him was a big part of my grant application when he laughed at our presentation.

I continued: "And second, if you don't loan us the money, it's just going to sit in your bank account drawing a little bit more interest. It'll become a bigger pile of money we both know you don't need right now. It won't change anyone's life. Or you can loan us the $70,000, help fund this dream, and bet on me that I'll pay you back." I then sat there in silence. I was more nervous than I had ever been in my entire life. Did I really just say all that out loud?

Jesse didn't hesitate a second. He smiled, "Tomorrow morning, come with me to the bank. I'll wire the money to your account."

With less than 24 hours before our flight to Africa, we had the money for our trip.

A few years later, I won the Young Alumni of the Year award for the University of Georgia. In a picture from the gala that evening, it shows the four of us who started Global L.E.A.D.—Robbie, Courtney, Kevin, and me. And in the middle of the picture is the man who made it all happen: Jesse Peel. When I won the UGA Business School annual award, I invited some special people to come and sit at my table: my Mom, my Dad, my brother Jeff, Kevin, Robbie, Courtney, and the one and only, Mr. Jesse Peel.

It took me three years to pay Jesse back, but I loved writing that check to him. We were completely out of resources, but we hadn't run out of resourcefulness. We refused to give up. We were motivated because we were living for something beyond money, beyond applause, and beyond comfort. We were captured by a purpose that was far bigger than ourselves, and it brought out the best in us.

What are the limits of your resources? Just remember: there are no limits to your resourcefulness. Keep dreaming, keep thinking, keep being creative. Find a way.

Not too long ago, Kevin and I reminisced about my meeting with Jesse Peel to ask him to loan us $70,000. Kevin gave that wry smile of his and told me, "That was before I knew you as well as I do now. I just trusted you with blind faith, but now that I look back on it, what you did was absolutely insane! You didn't really have a plan. You just went for it."

I couldn't have said it better myself. It took a truckload of pressure and 10 seconds of insane courage for me to make that phone call to Jesse. Then, when I met Jesse for dinner that night, I needed 10 more seconds of insane courage to verbalize the request.

Before you can jump in to a new level of resourcefulness, you probably need to jump out of the rat race of valuing your finite resources of intelligence, money, possessions, pleasure, or power. There are bigger, better things to live for, but we won't even look for a higher purpose unless we see the emptiness of our culture's attractions.

When the right purpose grips our hearts, something amazing occurs: We find ways to make it happen, we refuse to quit, we look for open doors we've never seen before, and we become incredibly creative. Nothing will stop us. Sure, people will say we're crazy, but that's okay. We'd rather be considered just a little odd than live a bland, tasteless existence.

But few of us can jump in alone. Like our team going to Africa, we need a "courage committee," a personal board of advisors who believe in us even if no one else does. We don't need a hundred such people, but we have to have at least one—one person, perhaps already in our lives, who would love to see us do something remarkable.

Look beyond your resources to your wit, your creativity, your dreams . . . your limitless possibilities. When you look at your bank account or investments, you feel discouraged. When you look in the mirror, you feel inadequate. When you look at your GPA, you probably realize you weren't the smartest in your class. These are the resource measuring sticks almost everyone else uses, but we need a different one: resourcefulness.

When I think back on my meeting with Jesse, I realize he had been only a few miles away all that time. I just didn't think of him until our backs were against the wall. We had been focused on the traditional ways of raising money. We didn't get really creative until those failed.

I'm convinced there are people around us who would love nothing more than to see us break through our limitations to do something great. Too often, we don't tap into their faith, love, and resources because our dreams aren't high enough to push us to be and do more. When our dreams outpace our resources, we have to become resourceful. Or to put it the other way around: if we don't feel pushed to be resourceful, our dreams probably aren't big enough to capture our hearts.

Desperation is uncomfortable, but it can bring out the very best in us. In those moments, we need 10 seconds of insane courage.

Fear says, "You don't have the resources to be successful."
Courage responds, "Your resourcefulness is worth more than any resources."

WHEN I'VE LOST MY WAY OR WHEN I AM CONFUSED

ABOUT A PATH TO TAKE, I REMEMBER THAT MOST

ANSWERS I NEED I ALREADY POSSESS—DEEP INSIDE.

I AM NATURALLY CREATIVE, RESOURCEFUL AND WHOLE.

IF I CONSULT MY INVISIBLE COMPASS,

I'LL KNOW WHAT TO DO.

—— *Steve Goodier*

CHAPTER 26

Real Treasure

A ll of us are treasure hunters. We search every day for the things we're sure will bring us the most happiness, applause, and power. Too often, though, the treasure we find is a sham, a counterfeit, dust and ashes. It looked so good that we devoted our lives to get it. We were driven, sacrificing everything for it, but in the end, it left us empty.

- Gatsby was fabulously rich, but he was miserable and lonely.

- Some of the most gorgeous supermodels say they feel fat and ugly.

- People who try to look cool can always find someone with nicer clothes and better hair.

- Geniuses are always looking over their shoulders at other brilliant people.

- No matter how much we get, it's never enough, can't satisfy us for very long, and always leaves us confused and frustrated. We need to find real treasure: a transcendent purpose that brings out the best in us, but without the toxic ingredients of comparison and competition.

We need to wake up. Many (if not most) of the messages in our culture are lies (or at least distortions of the truth and over-promising). When will we realize the promises are empty? When will we change direction and live for something more? There's nothing inherently wrong with wealth, popularity, power, and pleasure . . . as long as those things aren't in the center of our affections. If we can hold them with an open hand, enjoying them when we have them but not being crushed when we don't, they remain in their rightful, secondary place in our lives.

It's fascinating to watch young people and listen to older people. Most young people are drinking the Kool-Aid. They spend every waking moment pursuing things that don't last: money, stuff, thrills, and prestige. But a lot of older people have learned life's most important lessons: there are more important things in life.

The challenge for the old is to let the experiences of life, the good and the bad, lead to wisdom, and to avoid becoming cynical and bitter. The challenge of the young is to develop that wisdom much sooner, to live for a higher cause, and to let the secondary pursuits remain secondary.

YOU WILL BECOME WAY LESS CONCERNED WITH

WHAT OTHER PEOPLE THINK OF YOU

WHEN YOU REALIZE HOW SELDOM THEY DO.

——David Foster Wallace

10 Seconds Starts Now
ROAD TO COURAGE

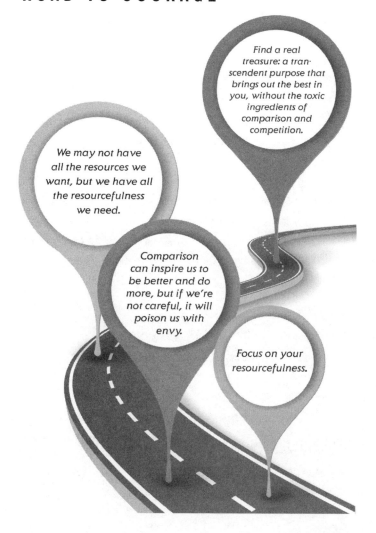

Find a real treasure: a transcendent purpose that brings out the best in you, without the toxic ingredients of comparison and competition.

We may not have all the resources we want, but we have all the resourcefulness we need.

Comparison can inspire us to be better and do more, but if we're not careful, it will poison us with envy.

Focus on your resourcefulness.

**FEAR SAYS,
"YOU DON'T HAVE THE RESOURCES TO BE SUCCESSFUL."**

**COURAGE RESPONDS,
"YOUR RESOURCEFULNESS IS WORTH MORE THAN ANY RESOURCES."**

FEAR FACTOR 7

Fear of Disappointing Others: *Affirmation Nation*

**FEAR SAYS,
"THEY'LL THINK I'M FOOLISH, INADEQUATE, OR DUMB."**

**COURAGE RESPONDS,
"THEY DON'T BUILD CONCRETE STATUES FOR CRITICS."**

CHAPTER 27

Pulling Strings

Everything in me wants to despise Tim Tebow. For those who aren't fans of SEC college football, my comment may sound startling, but people from the University of Georgia (Go Dawgs!) completely understand my sentiment. Only once in Tim's four years as the Florida Gators quarterback did the Dogs come out on top in their annual game in Jacksonville. In the last two years, we were stomped, trounced, humiliated. Tebow not only played well; he won the Heisman Trophy . . . at the expense of my beloved Bulldogs. To tell the truth, I want to despise him, but my admiration for him is almost boundless.

Unless you have never watched a football game in America, you know about Tim Tebow. He is an American phenomenon. It's obvious he doesn't live by pleasing people. He has taken stands and done things that make him a lightning rod of criticism. He is an outspoken Christian, which won praise from some corners and fierce ridicule from others. Plenty of people looked for any flaw, any misstep, any inconsistency so they could blast him. He seldom gave even the slightest opening for their fury.

The feature that amazes me more than anything is Tebow's unflinching willingness to keep moving forward, no matter what obstacles he faces or criticism he endures. He seems to live with a deep sense of security, as Henri Nouwen said we all should live, "beyond all human praise and blame."[29]

As a star quarterback at Florida, Tim was often in the national spotlight. He wrote the references of his favorite Bible verses on the black stripes under his eyes so the television cameras wouldn't miss his driving passion. In interviews, he talked easily and confidently about his faith as well as football. His athletic prowess and his leadership were honored with the highest award in the college game. As a sophomore, he led Florida to a National Championship, and he was named Most Valuable Player of the game. Fame, however, never went to his head.

After graduating, Tim was drafted by the Denver Broncos of the NFL and eventually traded to the New York Jets, where he sat on the bench most of the time. He was cut the next year and later ESPN hired Tim as a college football analyst. As it happened before, he received both praise and criticism for his work on television. He continued to work out so he would be ready for a football career, but the doors remained shut. In August of 2016, he announced he would try out for Major League Baseball. Yes, baseball, not football. A scout from the New York Mets thought he had enough potential to sign him to a minor league contract. He played well enough to be promoted through the minor league system, thrilling the fans with some towering home runs along the way. Of course, he wants to make it to the Major Leagues and have a sterling career, but if he doesn't, he'll be okay. The fear of disappointing others never seems to slow him down.

Beyond his tenacity to push through adversity and criticism, Tebow has shown a loving and compassionate heart. He has reached out to disadvantaged children, provided funds to build an orphanage, and helped raise money for a pediatric cancer center near the campus of the University of Florida. He regularly reaches out to kids with autism, Down Syndrome, and other disabilities.

Perspective. It's what makes Tim Tebow different. It's what defines him. It's what keeps him going. As he played baseball in the minor leagues, a reporter asked him about the pressure he felt during a batting slump. He explained, "So much of handling sports is handling pressure. But what pressure do you have if you're 0 for 12 at the plate versus someone who's fighting for their life, versus someone we picked up on the side of the street in Haiti because they're not wanted, or they're crippled, or they're thrown into the garbage? How do you compare those things? For me, there's not a comparison. That's why we pursue sports as a game. We can give our time and energy and effort to it, but at the end of the day, I know that's not why I'm here. It's not my biggest purpose. It's not my biggest calling. I don't want to be known as a football player or a baseball player. I want my life to be so much more than that. I want to be someone who was known for bringing faith, hope, and love to those needing a brighter day in their darkest hour of need. I'm grateful for sports because it has given me a platform to be able to share love and care for people all over the world, so I wouldn't trade that for anything."[30]

The reporter got more than he bargained for. He probably assumed Tebow would be distraught over his batting slump. Most of the world lives in Affirmation Nation, living and dying by the opinions of others. Tim Tebow obviously has a passport to another land.

Praise is intoxicating, and criticism can crush us. Tim Tebow shows us that a higher purpose can insulate us from the ravages of others' opinions of us, and at the same time, drive us to do something that really makes a difference.

Tim Tebow hasn't abandoned relationships. Far from it. But he has found a deeper sense of security, a strong identity, that enables him to connect with people without fearing them or manipulating them. He has learned the secret of healthy connections with people.

I believe human beings were created for relationships. We can't thrive without meaningful connections with people. And in fact, countless studies show that the breakdown of those connections leads to the full range of personal distresses, from anxiety, insecurity, and depression to isolation and suicidal thoughts and actions. Meaningful relationships aren't optional; they're required for the proper functioning of human beings.

This drive to be loved and accepted produces a strange blend of hope and fear. We long for a few people, even if it's only one person, to delight in us, to think we hung the moon, to accept us unconditionally. And at the same time, we're terrified that those we value won't value us. In this fear—or worse, in the conclusion that we've irretrievably lost the love we crave—we react in any of several ways: we try to earn others' approval by noticing what they need and giving it to them; we feel vulnerable, so we try to grab power and earn respect by intimidating and dominating others; or we shrink back from any perceived threat and desperately try to remain invisible and avoid rocking the boat. And of course, some of us use more than one approach to guard our hearts and fill the emptiness created by the absence of love and acceptance.

I believe there are two distinct—and distinctly different—motivations at play here. Those who are convinced they are loved, accepted, and valued can be wonderfully creative without the fear of losing the security they enjoy in their relationships. They live with a firm foundation, and they can build a life of love, joy, creativity, and courage on that solid foundation. But many more of us aren't convinced we're already completely accepted. We crave it, so we perform to earn it. Everything we do is as an actor on stage to please an audience . . . and we live and die by the reviews!

Some of us have dreams, but we hold back because we're so afraid we'll be criticized, or worse, ignored. And in this day of social media, we're assured we'll get the full range of responses. If we're insecure and live for approval, we can get 99 positive comments and one criticism, and we feel devastated instead of thrilled. On the other side, some are driven to do things to please people, to hear words of affirmation. Those people also live and die by every written word, spoken word, and facial expression they receive. Both holding back and being driven to please are sure signs we have a weak foundation.

I'm afraid we usually have the wrong solution to the problem. We try harder to be invisible and invulnerable, or we try harder to say the right words, do the right thing, wear the right clothes, and go the right places to win smiles and applause. But trying harder just keeps us running faster on the same treadmill.

The answer isn't to become a monk or a nun and renounce pleasure and success. (Nothing against monks or nuns, by the way.) We can still get out there and be involved with people, but we may need to address the fundamental condition of our hearts: Are we pleasing, proving, and hiding because we're trying to compensate for our insecurities, or are we free to be ourselves and do all kinds of things without hyper-analysis, fear, or defiance?

Are we trying to fill a hole, or are we free to be fully ourselves because we're sure we're loved and accepted? These aren't easy questions to answer. In fact, they may be the most challenging (and revealing) questions we'll ever ask.

There's absolutely nothing good and right about being obnoxious because we don't care what people think of us. That kind of person wants to look strong, but it reveals an inner weakness. And there's nothing wrong with enjoying plenty of likes when you post something crazy like wearing a tuxedo with penguins on an ice sheet in Antarctica . . . unless you're too affected by negative comments and the positive ones mean a little too much. This, too, is a sign of insecurity. Either way, we live in an Affirmation Nation. I'm asking you . . . and I'm demanding of me . . . that we at least ask the questions about why we do what we do.

THERE CAN BE NO VULNERABILITY WITHOUT RISK; THERE CAN BE NO COMMUNITY WITHOUT VULNERABILITY; THERE CAN BE NO PEACE, AND ULTIMATELY NO LIFE, WITHOUT COMMUNITY.

—M. Scott Peck

Strings

When we worry about what others think of us, the strings run both ways. We feel like puppets dancing to other people's opinions of us, and we try to pull their strings to get them to give us the respect and love we want. Here are some thoughts many of us have.

"I'm worried what my friends will think . . . especially *that* friend!"

"If people really knew me, they'd leave."

"I'm sure my colleagues think I'm arrogant or crazy."

"My boss controls my future, so I have to play by the company's rules."

"My wife [or husband] would never want me to risk our comfort or security."

"I'll change what I say so I can fit in: I'm a chameleon."

"I can't stand it if _____ doesn't like me."

"I must have the approval of _____ to feel good about myself."

"I have to prove myself by being bigger, better, and badder than anyone else."

CHAPTER 28

Looking In

A poem written in 1934 by Dale Wimbrow gives us a clear view into the importance and the fragility of our self-concepts. Ultimately, self-confidence is a treasured possession, one that can't be inflated and destroyed by praise or shattered by condemnation. One of the greatest gifts we can give ourselves is acceptance. The poem is called "The Guy in the Glass."

When you get what you want in your struggle for self,
And the world makes you King for a day,
Just go to the mirror and look at yourself,
And see what that man has to say.

For it isn't your Father, or Mother, or Wife,
Whose judgment upon you must pass,
The fellow whose verdict counts most in your life,
Is the one staring back from the glass.

He's the feller to please, never mind all the rest,
For he's with you, clear to the end,
And you've passed your most difficult, dangerous test
If the man in the glass is your friend. . . .

You can fool the whole world down the pathway of years,
And get pats on the back as you pass,
But your final reward will be heartache and tears
If you've cheated the man in the glass.[31]

THE REFLECTION

So, is the person looking back from the mirror your friend? Or do you feel inferior because you don't believe you measure up, or perhaps superior because you're doing better than others? Is the verdict of your life in others' hands? If it is, you'll always feel insecure, always worry about others' opinions, and always look for ways to please, prove, or hide.

I have to find a source of inner confidence so I can wear my tuxedo on my next trip and thoroughly enjoy posting a picture of it without too much fear or too much hope. But I also need to find a source of strength so I'm not too inflated when people praise a talk I give, or down in the dumps if they find too many things wrong with it.

I plan to keep wearing the tuxedo wherever I go. I enjoy it. I plan to keep giving talks I hope will challenge and inspire people. I think it's my calling and purpose in life. Whatever people think and say about me, I have to be big enough and strong enough to listen carefully to their input but not be destroyed by correction. I want to be as real as I can be and let people respond however they want to respond.

Will we ever get to a place where we're so secure we aren't the least bit inflated by praise or hurt by criticism? No, not in this life. We're thoroughly human, and we all have insecurities and fears. Admit them and embrace them. Part of being alive is being aware of the common struggle to be real, to create a life worth living, and to find people who will run through it with us. We'll never be able to please everybody, but we can have a few wonderful, warm relationships with people who matter more than life itself. That's what really counts. We need to cut the strings that we've let people pull to make us dance to their tunes, and we need to cut the ones we've been trying to pull to get people to treat us the way we want to be treated. No more games, no more strings, no more masks to hide who we really are . . . at least with a few people.

Look in the mirror, find out who you really are, and treasure the connections with those who truly value you. If you don't have any of those people, don't stop until you find one or two. You can't really live without them.

Find those people, places, and things that make you come alive. I have a few really close friends who provide the stability I need so I can be completely me. They encourage me to do the things that make me come alive. When I travel, especially to far out places like North Korea, Cuba, and Easter Island, I wonder myself what I'm doing—and I sometimes wonder if I'll make it out of there! But going there, with my tux in hand, makes me come alive. If people notice it and laugh, or stare, or are just confused, then that's okay; I know I've put just a little something in their day, something they can tell their friends about, and maybe something that will propel them to be a little more alive, too.

"ANYWAY"

A poem written by Kent M. Keith was reportedly inscribed on the walls of Mother Teresa's children's home in Calcutta, India. The poem describes our insight into the pressures we often feel in relationships, and it articulates our courageous responses. It's called "Anyway."

People are often unreasonable, illogical and self-centered;
Forgive them anyway.

If you are kind, people may accuse you of selfish,
ulterior motives;
Be kind anyway.

If you are successful, you will win some false friends
and some true enemies;
Succeed anyway.

If you are honest and frank, people may cheat you;
Be honest and frank anyway.

What you spend years building, someone could
destroy overnight;
Build anyway.

If you find serenity and happiness, they may be jealous;
Be happy anyway.

The good you do today, people will often forget tomorrow;
Do good anyway.

Give the world the best you have, and it may never be enough;
Give the world the best you've got anyway.

You see, in the final analysis, it is between you and your God;
It was never between you and them anyway.[32]

It'll be hard to face the fear of disappointing others, find your-self, learn to be yourself, and face your critics, but be strong and do it anyway.

THREE NEEDS

We can't overcome the fear of disappointing others by "read-ing" their moods and changing our words and actions to please them. We only conquer it by having a dream that's much bigger than our fear. When Matthew McConaughey won 2014's Best Actor Oscar for his role in *Dallas Buyers Club*, he took the op-portunity to communicate his philosophy of life and his driving purpose. He thanked the Academy and the film's director and ac-tors. Then he told the audience there are three things he needs each day: "One of them is something to look up to, another is something to look forward to, and another is someone to chase." He looks up to God, who "has graced my life with opportuni-ties that I know are not of my hand or any other human hand." He looks forward to his family—someday enjoying a reunion in heaven with his father, his mother who was in the audience that night, his two older brothers, his wife Camila and their children. He then said he's chasing his hero, actually, an image of himself as a hero for others. He doesn't expect to ever actually become that hero, but the chase is still worthwhile.

He ended his address in typical style: "So, to any of us, whatever those things are, whatever it is we look up to, whatever it is we look forward to, and whoever it is we're chasing. To that I say: Amen. To that I say, All right, all right, all right. To that I say, just keep living, eh? Thank you."[33]

If we look at others through the lens of the fear of disappointing them, we'll be either hesitant or driven . . . or some strange blend of both . . . and always anxious. But when we find a stronger sense of security and significance, we begin to see people the way McConaughey does: We look up to God and thank him for his great grace, we look forward to meaningful interactions with those we love, and we chase the dream of making a difference in the lives of others. We want to be heroes for their sakes, not to impress them or have control over them, but only because we have an unfiltered, open-handed love for them.

Is that even possible? Yes. It takes 10 seconds of insane courage to be honest about the fear, find enough security to be find yourself and be yourself, and then be courageous to keep pressing into love and creativity even when others think you're nuts.

PEOPLE WITH DEEP AND LASTING FRIENDSHIPS MAY BE INTROVERTS, EXTROVERTS, YOUNG, OLD, DULL, INTELLIGENT, HOMELY, GOOD-LOOKING; BUT THE ONE CHARACTERISTIC THEY ALWAYS HAVE IN COMMON IS OPENNESS.

——Alan Loy McGinnis

A Different View

We all thrive on meaningful connections with people, but we need healthy independence from the bondage of pleasing people and getting our worth from their opinion of us. We need to have a different perspective on the way our family, friends, and colleagues view us.

Your friends aren't your friends unless they celebrate who you really are.

Your spouse wants to be married to someone who chases dreams.

Your colleagues may not know your dreams. Find one or two you can trust, and share your heart.

Your boss actually is looking for your best ideas.

Your family wants safety and security, not necessarily adventure. You may need to push them a little to really live!

And you can tell yourself:

"I can make better decisions about who to trust."

"I can break the pattern of trusting the wrong people or not trusting at all."

"I can find enough security to be who I really am."

"I don't need everyone's approval, but I need someone's."

"I'm going to cut the strings of unrealistic and unhealthy expectations people have of me."

"I'm going to cut the strings of manipulation I try to pull in my relationships with others."

CHAPTER 29

Jump Out

As a kid in school I always had one answer for what I wanted to be when I grew up: James Bond. I don't think I realized he wasn't a real person, nor did I understand this wasn't an actual career path. I am really skinny and my adventures growing up consisted of whiffle ball in the back yard. When I finally donned my first tuxedo, there was no mention of 007. Oh well.

After I started traveling, I had the idea to be my own slimmed down version of my childhood hero and take pictures at the world's most iconic landmarks with me wearing a tux. And so I did. Traveling became a personal adventure and my carry-on always included one thing: my tux. I decided to just go for it regardless of ridicule and suited up for photos on a camel in front of the Pyramids (in a tux), atop Machu Picchu (in a tux), jumping off the Great Wall of China (in a tux), and standing alongside those alien statues on Easter Island (once again, in a tux). It became my go-to wherever I went. I didn't mind jumping out and making a splash . . . or maybe making a fool of myself!

On my 30th birthday, I visited my seventh (and final) continent: Antarctica. As our ship sailed past a huge iceberg and pulled up next to an ice sheet, I climbed off wearing my tux and walked out among the penguins along with my good friend Grant Zarzour, who had a camera in hand. The picture of me that day is hilarious . . . and ridiculous. I didn't care who thought I was crazy or if they really believed I thought I looked like James Bond.

I just wanted to be myself and found one friend who would put up with the shenanigans. A big thanks to Grant for those very first tuxedo pics alongside the penguins from the icy cold continent of Antarctica.

I uploaded the pictures to social media, and people (at least those who responded) got a kick out of them. On the way back, I met my brother Jeff in Peru to hike Machu Picchu together. When we got to the Inca Trail, I still had my tuxedo. It may have smelled like the penguins, but Jeff didn't care. I wore it for part of the hike . . . long enough to entertain those I passed on the trail and to take a few pictures overlooking Machu Picchu.

Again, I posted the pictures and people responded . . . mostly positively. Many of them used words like "hilarious" and "ridiculous" in their posts. That was entirely appropriate.

My decision to wear a tux at historic sites around the world began as a personal endeavor, but it morphed into "affirmation nation" when people responded so positively. I wasn't sure if I'd get likes or snarks, but now, I wear the tux at places all over the world wherever I travel. At this point it's more wondering where will the tux show up next. A bit more *Where's Waldo* and a little less James Bond, but it's fun. It's nothing more than that, but that's good enough for me. Every now and then, someone posts a really negative comment about my sanity or lack of good taste, but at this point, it's all good. The images of me in a tux have become part of who I am: not James Bond, but Garrett Gravesen. People will like it or not. I'm okay being me . . . and that's a really, really good thing.

Earning approval . . . wearing masks to impress and hide . . . saying things we don't mean . . . living in fear of an unkind word or a raised eyebrow . . . wondering what people are saying about us . . . reliving conversations and beating ourselves up because we said something stupid . . . changing our values to please the person in front of us—these are just a few of the ways we lose ourselves when we're afraid of disappointing the people we respect. We need 10 seconds of insane courage to make different decisions about how to think, speak, and act like secure, confident people. But before those pivotal moments, we need to accomplish one more tasks: We need to *find* ourselves before we can learn to *be* ourselves.

Many of us have been playing a role so long that we have no idea who we really are. We've tried to fit in. We've tailored every aspect of our lives so people would think we're cool and okay, and in all of our careful analysis and miniscule adjustments to be acceptable, we don't even know what we really love. In the past, we looked in the mirror and saw someone who looked and acted in a way that won approval—or tried to, anyway. Now, we may look in the mirror and see a fraud. That's not a bad thing. Actually, it's progress.

The next step is the hard one. We need to find the courage to dig even deeper to uncover who we really are. That means we'll need an authentic friend who can help us—someone who won't tell us what we *want* to hear, but will tell us what we *need* to hear. We've tried desperately to appear desirable and competent. Now we find someone who really believes we're desirable and competent. That's a true friend. Gradually, over time, we'll probably realize two things: we've drowned some parts of our personality and desires under a flood of misplaced devotions to people, and there are some hidden parts of us that have been waiting to come to life!

As we find ourselves, we have plenty of opportunities to be ourselves. We speak up when we want to and we shut up when we need to . . . and we have the sense to know the difference. We celebrate our uniqueness, and we don't feel compelled to fit in at all costs. But we also don't feel compelled to be different just to defy those who are pressuring us to conform. Slowly, we find ways to rise above the external pressure that has crushed us so long.

In each of these moments, we're more creative, less confined, bolder, and less fearful than before. But make no mistake: everything in us has been programmed to keep living in the fear of disapproval, and at least some of our existing relationships are with people who much prefer that we'd keep playing games and wearing masks. If we live in truth, it exposes their phoniness, and they don't like that one bit!

Pastor Andy Stanley talks about a caged gorilla to illustrate the courage needed to face a big change, a change like the one we're addressing in this chapter. He said, "If there is an issue you want to avoid, you go to the cage, open it up and invite [the gorilla] into the room."[34]

Becoming vulnerable enough to expose our deepest insecurities is opening the cage and letting the gorilla out. It's scary, and we're never quite sure what's going to happen. If we keep the cage closed, we can study it for years, but nothing will ever change. There won't be a life-changing encounter.

Find yourself, be yourself, and then, get ready for the critics. They'll always be there. The people who will be most critical of your new life will be those who have tried to control you, those who used you, and those who avoided blame and responsibility by pushing these onto you. When you change, they'll try to push you back into your old mold. Be ready for their pressure. Don't be surprised. It's coming.

How have you reacted to them in the past when you tried to change? Have you caved in to their demands? Have you tried to hide from them? Have you become belligerent and defiant? It's time to create a new pattern of responses: communicate with truth and grace. Depending on the relationship and the situation, sometimes it's best to ignore them and move on to other people you can trust. But in our most important relationships, we need to explain that we're learning a different way to live, and things are going to be different. Speak calmly but clearly, and don't back down. In the most difficult situations, you'll need help from a counselor or a good friend with experience in difficult relationships. There will be times when you're confused. There will be times when you'll want to go back to the way things were before. Don't cave in.

Face the haters, take the heat, and stay strong. In relationships, you'll have plenty of moments when you need 10 seconds of insane courage. Remember, they don't build concrete statues for critics.

Fear says, "They'll think I'm foolish, inadequate, or dumb."
Courage responds, "They don't build concrete statues
for critics."

OUR DEEPEST FEAR IS NOT THAT WE ARE INADEQUATE.
OUR DEEPEST FEAR IS THAT WE ARE POWERFUL BEYOND
MEASURE. IT IS OUR LIGHT, NOT OUR DARKNESS THAT
MOST FRIGHTENS US. WE ASK OURSELVES, WHO AM I
TO BE BRILLIANT, GORGEOUS, TALENTED, FABULOUS?
ACTUALLY, WHO ARE YOU *NOT* TO BE? YOU ARE A CHILD OF
GOD. YOUR PLAYING SMALL DOES NOT SERVE THE WORLD.
THERE IS NOTHING ENLIGHTENED ABOUT SHRINKING SO
THAT OTHER PEOPLE WON'T FEEL INSECURE AROUND
YOU. WE ARE ALL MEANT TO SHINE, AS CHILDREN DO.
WE WERE BORN TO MAKE MANIFEST THE GLORY OF GOD
THAT IS WITHIN US. IT'S NOT JUST IN SOME OF US; IT'S IN
EVERYONE. AND AS WE LET OUR OWN LIGHT SHINE, WE
UNCONSCIOUSLY GIVE OTHER PEOPLE PERMISSION TO DO
THE SAME. AS WE ARE LIBERATED FROM OUR OWN FEAR,
OUR PRESENCE AUTOMATICALLY LIBERATES OTHERS.

— *Marianne Williamson,* A Return to Love

The Courage to be Honest

You and I face 10 seconds of insane courage every time . . .

Someone asks a personal question and we tell the truth.

We say "yes" when we want to say "yes."

We say "no" when we want to say "no."

We stop trusting untrustworthy people.

We refuse to second-guess everything we think, say, and do.

We find at least one person we can trust with our secrets.

We learn to laugh more easily.

We can cry more deeply.

We're free to pursue our dreams.

We celebrate others' successes as much as our own.

We feel comfortable in our own skin.

We like ourselves.

CHAPTER 30

Connected but Not Consumed

All of us have concerns in our relationships. Our connections with others are supremely important, but they're also immensely complicated. As we grow wiser and stronger, our reaction to the difficulties is no longer to isolate and hope the problems go away, intimidate others to make them controllable, or try desperately to fit in and be accepted. It's time to change, and as we change internally to become more secure and confident, we also learn to relate to people in healthy ways.

When we're more secure, we can be more authentic. Other people may play games, but we speak the truth in love. In staff meetings when someone gives a presentation or report, others may be afraid of hurting the person's feelings with constructive criticism, but we're learning to say what needs to be said without the toxic drip of arrogance and disdain. If we say things that are true, with kindness in our voices, the atmosphere in the room can change. It may not happen overnight . . . it *won't* happen overnight! But it can happen.

We want our light to shine, and we want everyone else's light to shine too. We go from being competitors—with our spouse, siblings, colleagues, and friends—to being coaches and cheerleaders. People don't always want to hear the truth. We didn't want to hear it either when we were insecure. But they'll learn to appreciate the fact that we tell it like it is, and we say it because we truly want the best for them. That's powerful. That's incredible. That's life changing for everybody.

IT IS NOT THE CRITIC WHO COUNTS; NOT THE MAN WHO POINTS OUT HOW THE STRONG MAN STUMBLES, OR WHERE THE DOER OF DEEDS COULD HAVE DONE THEM BETTER. THE CREDIT BELONGS TO THE MAN WHO IS ACTUALLY IN THE ARENA, WHOSE FACE IS MARRED BY DUST AND SWEAT AND BLOOD; WHO STRIVES VALIANTLY; WHO ERRS, WHO COMES SHORT AGAIN AND AGAIN, BECAUSE THERE IS NO EFFORT WITHOUT ERROR AND SHORTCOMING; BUT WHO DOES ACTUALLY STRIVE TO DO THE DEEDS; WHO KNOWS GREAT ENTHUSIASMS, THE GREAT DEVOTIONS; WHO SPENDS HIMSELF IN A WORTHY CAUSE; WHO AT THE BEST KNOWS IN THE END THE TRIUMPH OF HIGH ACHIEVEMENT, AND WHO AT THE WORST, IF HE FAILS, AT LEAST FAILS WHILE DARING GREATLY, SO THAT HIS PLACE SHALL NEVER BE WITH THOSE COLD AND TIMID SOULS WHO NEITHER KNOW VICTORY NOR DEFEAT.

—*Theodore Roosevelt*

10 Seconds Starts Now
ROAD TO COURAGE

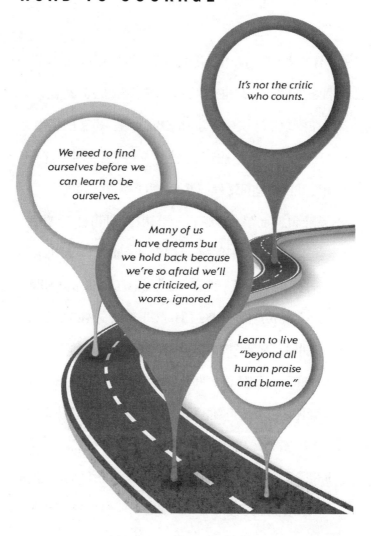

It's not the critic who counts.

We need to find ourselves before we can learn to be ourselves.

Many of us have dreams but we hold back because we're so afraid we'll be criticized, or worse, ignored.

Learn to live "beyond all human praise and blame."

FEAR SAYS,
"THEY'LL THINK I'M FOOLISH, INADEQUATE, OR DUMB."

COURAGE RESPONDS,
"THEY DON'T BUILD CONCRETE STATUES FOR CRITICS."

FEAR FACTOR 8

Fear of Failure:
It's Never Forever

**FEAR SAYS,
"YOU'LL BE DEFINED BY YOUR FAILURE."**

**COURAGE RESPONDS,
"GET GOING. FAILURE ISN'T FINAL."**

CHAPTER 31

Not the End of the World

ara Blakely's father redefined failure for her. In an interview with CNN's Anderson Cooper, she explained, "Instead of failure being the outcome, failure became not trying. It forced me at a young age to want to push myself so much further out of my comfort zone." Her conclusion was simple and breathtaking: If you're not failing, you're not growing.

Sara's father is an attorney, and her mother is an artist. She planned to go to law school, but she didn't make high enough scores on her LSAT. Instead, she went to work for Disney World, and she had a second job as a standup comic. Soon she got a job selling fax machines door-to-door, and she realized she was really good at sales. In fact, the company promoted her to national sales trainer when she was only 25.

A couple of years later, she stood in front of her mirror as she tried to choose clothes for a party that night. She wanted to wear a particular pair of pants, but they didn't fit quite right. In an interview at *Inc.* Magazine's 2011 Women's Summit, she explained her conundrum: "We had the traditional shapers that were so thick, and left lines or bulges on the thigh. And then we had the underwear which leaves a panty line. . . . And then came along the thong, which still confuses me because all that did was put underwear exactly where we had been trying to get it out of."

Sara cut the feet out of some pantyhose and put them on. They firmed up her shape without being bulky or showing lines. It was the first iteration of a brand-new product and a new purpose for her career.

Sara soon relocated to Atlanta. She was still selling fax machines, but now she had a dream to fulfill. She had only $5,000 to invest in her idea, and she soon learned virtually all of that money would need to go to a patent attorney's fees. Instead, she bought a book at a local bookstore and wrote her own patent application.

She drove to North Carolina to meet with executives of hosiery mills, but none of them bought into her vision. Failure after failure? Her dad would be proud of her! Finally, a mill operator in Asheboro called to tell her that his three daughters saw potential in her concept. For over a year, she perfected her design, trying them out on family and friends. During that year, she decided on the name of her company: Spanx.

Sara thought long and hard about the name of her company. Years later, she recalled, "The name Spanx came while I was sitting in traffic in Atlanta, after a year of really bad names I had come up with. I knew that Kodak and Coca-Cola were two of the most recognized names in the world and they both have a strong 'K' sound. And some friends of mine who are standup comedians have told me that the 'K' sound makes the audience laugh. As soon as I decided that I wanted the name to have the 'K' sound for good luck, Spanx just appeared before my eyes and I pulled off the side of the road and wrote it down. I went home that night and trademarked it online for $150 with my credit card."[35]

She met with a representative of Neiman Marcus. If Neiman Marcus would carry her product, the sky would be the limit. The company rep must have looked skeptical, but Sara had an idea: she mustered 10 seconds of insane courage. She stepped into the ladies' room, put on her Spanx, and stepped out to demonstrate the difference it made in her own figure. The rep was impressed and put the product in seven stores. Soon, Bloomingdales, Saks, and Bergdorf Goodman carried Spanx. Sara handled virtually every aspect of the business operations, and she met as many failures as successes. Blakely's $5,000 investment resulted in her becoming the youngest self-made female billionaire . . . so we can assume she has learned a lot from her failures!

Sara can look back at her father's influence on her perspective and tenacity. When kids come home from school, most parents ask, "Did you have a good day? What did you learn?" But Sara's father asked night after night, "What did you fail at today?" When she couldn't tell him about a specific failure, he was disappointed. Failure, she learned, is the pathway to success.[36]

I've had the pleasure of knowing Sara (we both live in Atlanta), and I've seen how her dad's perspective on failure has given her incredible confidence and courage. When failure becomes a friend, wide doors of opportunity open in front of us.

Ultimately, all the other fears are based on the terrifying prospect that personal failure will define us, ruin us, and stamp us with the irretrievable label of "loser." Failure seems final. Failure looks fatal. Failure looks like the end of the world as we know it. We're sure failure is the scarlet letter that shouts to every person we meet that we don't measure up.

Most of the people who wrestle with this fear construct their lives—their careers, their relationships, their hobbies, and every other detail of their existence—to prevent (or at least limit) any risk of failure. Oh, they enjoy their successes, even if they secretly know those were scaled back because they couldn't let themselves go for bigger wins. And besides, each success feels so good, such a huge relief, that they don't want to risk losses that would tarnish their reputations.

The fear of failure has both an internal and an external component. Many of us are haunted by past failures—either one that was so bad it's a permanently open wound or a recurring pattern of the same failure that we can't shake. The internal conclusions shape our external choices: Every time we face a new challenge, a new opportunity, a new risk, memories of that single event or the habit haunts us. The memories become more vivid, more real, more compelling than the open door in front of us, and we're stopped in our tracks.

Strangely, we can also be haunted by past successes. We got a rush from those occasions, and our reputations were built on them. When we're faced with new opportunities, we avoid them because we can't risk our self-image being diminished.

Either way, our minds today are haunted by the past.

It's not only our self-image we're afraid of ruining by another failure. We're sure people are watching, eager to criticize us and gleeful as they point out every flaw in our character or performance. The fear of failure, then, is all-encompassing, all-consuming, and completely devastating. When this fear blasts into our thoughts, we believe we're on the precipice of the end of the world.

FAILURE IS SO IMPORTANT. WE SPEAK ABOUT SUCCESS ALL THE TIME. IT IS THE ABILITY TO RESIST FAILURE OR USE FAILURE THAT OFTEN LEADS TO GREATER SUCCESS. I'VE MET PEOPLE WHO DON'T WANT TO TRY FOR FEAR OF FAILING.

—*J.K. Rowling*

It's Inevitable

When we're haunted by past failure, we bring our fears into every moment of the day. We're absolutely sure these statements we tell ourselves are true.

"If I fail, I'll never get another job in this field."

"Past screw-ups have defined me."

"Most ideas don't work anyway. There's no use in trying."

"It's far safer for me to climb the corporate ladder than try something on my own."

"It's scary, risky, crazy."

"Everybody around me is more competent and smarter than I am."

"I can't believe how badly I've messed up. If anyone knew . . ."

"I don't have any abilities that impress people."

"I spend all my time comparing myself to others . . . and coming up short."

"My strengths are limited but my weaknesses are huge."

CHAPTER 32

Redefining Failure

One of the most common—and most devastating—evidences of this fear is "catastrophizing." Psychologists say that this response has two components: first, imagining a negative outcome of any situation or choice and drawing the conclusion that this negative outcome will be catastrophic, and second, there's nothing the person can do about it.[37] The examples are as many and as varied as the events that happen to us daily:

- A wife imagines her husband's coolness means he doesn't care for her any more . . . and in fact, he's probably having an affair. Divorce is imminent, which will inevitably lead to poverty.

- A single guy hasn't had a date in three weeks, and he concludes he'll be alone for the rest of his life.

- A worker makes a mistake and assumes he'll be fired, he'll never get another job, and he'll end up on the street.

- A person has a routine physical. When the doctor's nurse calls back to schedule a phone consult with the doctor, the person's mind goes wild with thoughts about the most dreaded diseases.

- A young woman didn't get an invitation to a friend's party. She immediately believes she said or did something that was so offensive she's now an outsider. At first, she's confused about what the cause may be, but then she thinks of a dozen reasons she could be shunned.

- The new product's sales don't meet projections, so the sales manager wonders if he'll lose his job, will get a bad reference from his boss, and will have to get a job as a janitor . . . if that's even open to him after this career bomb.

These aren't merely hypothetical situations. *Business Insider* collected a list of leaders who are known for their success but failed spectacularly early in their careers:

- Walt Disney was fired by a Kansas City newspaper because the editor believed he "lacked imagination and had no good ideas."

- Oprah Winfrey was fired from her first job as a television news anchor because she was "too emotionally invested in her stories."

- Steven Spielberg was rejected several times by the University of Southern California School of Cinematic Arts.

- Isaac Newton's mother took him out of school so he could run the family farm. He was a miserable farmer.

- Vera Wang failed in her attempt to make the U.S. Olympic figure skating team. She went to work for *Vogue*, but didn't become the editor-in-chief, so she began designing clothes.

- Thomas Edison's teachers complained that he was "too stupid to learn anything."

- Fred Astaire auditioned for a film role, but the executive commented: "Can't sing. Can't act. Slightly balding. Can dance a little."

- Vincent Van Gogh sold only one painting during his lifetime.
- Theodor Seuss Geisel, known as Dr. Seuss, was rejected by 27 publishers when he submitted his first book.[38]

Every startup looks squarely into the face of failure. Every executive makes decisions that carry significant risk of not hitting the goal. Every employee has responsibilities that inherently carry the potential of screwing up. Every relationship that goes beyond the superficial opens a door to heartache. If we insist on avoiding failure at all costs, we'll live drab, empty, boring lives. If we're breathing, the risk of failure is a given.

Resilient people expect ups and downs, but fragile people can't handle failure because they believe it's a permanent stain on their reputations. Every person I know who has taken significant strides in life—in business, education, serving others, medicine, sports, marriage, friendships, parenting, and all other endeavors—can point to a string of failures, sometimes colossal failures, but they didn't let those setbacks become roadblocks.

Why do so many people root for Elon Musk's success? I don't know of any other billionaires who have so many people emotionally invested in their success. I think it's because Musk puts it all out there all the time. He lives on the edge. Sometimes his rockets explode, so we're thrilled when they fly. Sometimes the rockets land perfectly on the platform, and other times they miss the target and sink in the ocean. We root for his wins because we admire his courage in his losses. It's the same for you and me—though on a somewhat smaller scale! People root for us when we show the courage to get up after we've been knocked down and give it another try.

No, we're not all Elon Musk, but we all face the specter of failure over and over again in our relationships and careers. We may not be looking at billion-dollar risks, but the ones we face feel just as daunting.

If you're haunted by a single past failure that's so big you can't forget it, or if you've experienced a long string of the same failures, every painful, crippling memory is an opportunity for 10 seconds of insane courage to tell yourself, "That doesn't define me. I'm better than that."

If you have an idea but you're afraid to say it because you don't want any criticism, you can muster 10 seconds of insane courage to open your mouth and speak the first sentence. The rest will follow.

If you're in a relationship with someone who points out real or perceived failures in an attempt to control you, use your 10 seconds of insane courage to at least refute the accusation in your own mind . . . and find 10 seconds of insane courage to ask a mentor how to deal with the problem. Then you'll need another shot of courage to speak the truth to the offensive person and face the pushback.

If you want to rise to the next level of your organization, you'll need 10 seconds of insane courage to ask your supervisor what training and skills you need to take that step. And you'll need courage to face your peers who may question your motives.

If you want to create a new product, a new process, or a new business, you'll need 10 seconds of insane courage to sign the papers and launch the venture, and you'll need many more moments of courage as you experience the highs and lows.

Face the reality of past failures—and the real prospect of failure in every courageous choice—and find the inner strength to live for progress, not perfection.

I'VE COME TO BELIEVE THAT ALL MY PAST FAILURE
AND FRUSTRATION WERE ACTUALLY LAYING THE
FOUNDATION FOR THE UNDERSTANDINGS THAT HAVE
CREATED THE NEW LEVEL OF LIVING I NOW ENJOY.

—*Tony Robbins*

Patience, Persistence, and Perseverance

Failure is a downer . . . no doubt about it. But it's never forever. We can learn, we can rebound, we can grow stronger, wiser, and more humble. When we face failure, we need to remember:

A setback is often step 1 in a long process toward success.

Failure does not define you.

A singular failure doesn't make you a long-term loser.

Your best plans may not work, and that's okay.

Success is defined in different ways.

Patience is a paramount virtue.

Spectacular failures can lead to spectacular progress.

Failure often forces creativity.

If you can't let yourself fail, you won't learn.

CHAPTER 33

Jumping to Harvard . . . for the 15th Time

When I was in high school, my girlfriend and I both wanted to go to Harvard. Guess who got in? Not this guy.

My desire to go to Harvard, though, wasn't dead. In fact, it was alive and well. In the fall of my freshman year at the University of Georgia, I sold all my football tickets so I could buy a plane ticket to Boston to see my girlfriend . . . and set foot on Harvard's campus in Cambridge for the first time.

On my last night there, she introduced me to a group of her friends. As we sat on the steps at Widener Library, a cool fall breeze felt like a different world compared to the Athens, Georgia I'd left a couple of days before. As we talked, I asked each friend how they got into the school. All of them had graduated at the top of their high school class. That fact was so obvious no one even mentioned it. One of them had won a prestigious national science award, another made a perfect score on the SAT, and another was one of the most talented musicians in America—she had picked Harvard over Julliard.

After a while, one of them turned to me and asked, "So Garrett, what about you? What have you ever done?"

For the first time in my life, I had nothing to say. I felt completely lost for words.

By the end of that year, the distance from my girlfriend caused our relationship to grow stale, and we broke up. However, I always thought it had something to do with not getting into Hahhhhvard. As with all young love, it drove me into the arms of another. That other became Harvard itself. I made a solemn commitment that someday I'd become a student at Harvard and graduate. I didn't care if I got into the school of archeology or gardening, law or basket weaving. I just wanted to be able to attend what I considered (and still consider) the premier institution of learning in the world. This moment was one of my 10 seconds of insane courage to face the fact that I wasn't what I wanted to be, but failure wasn't forever.

I visited Harvard a few times over the next few years. When I was the UGA student body president, I took the freshmen coming into student government on a retreat to Harvard. The fifteen of us snuck into a class, met Natalie Portman, who was a student at the time, and walked around Harvard Yard to get a feel for the place. I told them, "You're all smart enough and resourceful enough to get into a school like Harvard one day." I was projecting my desire onto them, and hopefully, inspiring them to think, dream, and plan a little bigger.

After college, I even flew up to Harvard a few times for graduation. Yes, I could probably read the transcripts of the commencement speakers a week or two later, or maybe even see the video of graduation exercises, but I wanted to be there. I heard Bill Clinton, Bill Gates, J.K. Rowling, and other amazing people speak at commencement and launch the best and brightest into their careers.

About ten years after I graduated from Georgia, I decided to fill out an application to Harvard Business School. I got the letter that began, "Dear Mr. Gravesen, we regret to inform you . . ."

After Kevin and I had worked at Global L.E.A.D., we co-founded ADDO, a leadership consulting firm. We partnered with Chick-fil-A and created a national leadership program—Chick-fil-A Leader Academy. During a meeting with one of the company's executives, he told me about a program he'd attended at Harvard Business School designed for executives and entrepreneurs at least ten years past graduation. I fit the description perfectly, or so I thought. He offered to write a recommendation for me. My application included a detailed account of my life's story, including the internship with Merrill Lynch in Hong Kong, meeting Martin at the orphanage in Kenya, starting H.E.R.O. for Children, Global L.E.A.D., ADDO, and all the rest. It has to be the most ridiculous, outlandish application Harvard Business School has ever received—totally unvarnished and completely real.

I got accepted. I was thrilled to be at Harvard Business School, and even more, in their executive Program for Leadership Development. One of the projects I worked on in my studies was called "The Dash Project." When you look at a tombstone, you see the year the person was born and the year they died. In between is a small mark that represents everything in the person's life between those bookends. A famous poem called "The Dash" explains that the dash is the symbol of meaning or emptiness, contribution or passivity, courage or timidity. In the end, it won't matter what cars we drove, how nice our houses were, and how much pleasure we pursued. The only things that will matter are the moments we chose courage over comfort and love over fear. When we invest in the lives of others, our dash matters.

Mark Twain once said, "Twenty years from now you will be more disappointed by the things you didn't do than by the ones you did do. So throw off the bowlines. Sail away from the safe harbor. Catch the trade winds in your sails. Explore. Dream. Discover."[39] He was right.

What drives us? What captures our hearts? Sadly, for many of us, little if anything. I'm afraid the proliferation of dramatic events in the news every day—whether we receive it online, in the papers, or on television—has numbed us to the pain around us. We just can't absorb all the heartache, so we harden our hearts. The answer, though, isn't to avoid the reports. Instead, we need to slow down, imagine the plight of the suffering people, and let their situations break our hearts. Then we'll have the passion and drive to do something about it.

The Harvard Business School professors and students who were going to be the top leaders in the business world immediately got "the dash" and realized they were made for more than money, fame, and power.

As graduation approached, I had an idea to capture the essence of the men and women in our class. One of my classmates, Kevin Swiss, was a professional photographer and the best I had ever seen. He offered to partner on this together with me and take a photo of each person in our class in front of one of the classic chalkboards with professors' formulas and scribblings as the background. Over the course of two weeks, with the help of Kevin, other classmates, and the unwavering support of my section mates in 7B (big thanks to Casey, Niyantri, Elena, Javier, Arnault, Cumesh, and Vlad), we scheduled the shoots. I asked each one what they wanted to do with the rest of their lives— what they wanted their dash to represent. We aptly called it "The Dash Project." Our symbol was a piece of chalk turned sideways, which looked like a Dash when photographed against the chalkboard. We recorded their dreams, which were posted with their pictures on LED boards on campus. Harvard Business School has a similar project called "The Portrait Project" with black and white photography answering a meaningful question. It's amazing. We were excited that the Dash Project similarly took off with our executive program to highlight the hopes and dreams of our classmates, and the impact they plan to make.

I was selected by my classmates to be the class speaker at graduation. In my speech, I told them about the fifteen times I'd visited Harvard—and all the hopes and all the disappointments along the way. I told them that it's not always the people with the most prestige and power who make the biggest impact on our lives. And then I shared a story: "Once upon a time a teacher gave a test. It was a test unlike any other. These were some of the smartest students from all over the world. They all took the exact same test and when they got to the last question, they were all stumped. One student stared at it, then laughed and raised his hand. He was confused. He asked the professor, 'Does the last question actually count toward our grade?' The professor told the class, 'I want everyone to put down your pens and papers. There's an important lesson to be learned.' The last question simply said: What is the name of the person who cleans this classroom?"

Not a single student could answer the question. Not one. The professor continued, "A lot of people come into your life. All of them are important. It's your job to at least get to know their names and who they are."

I told our fellow graduates, "Here at Harvard Business School, his name is Vladimir. He cleans the blackboards after every class. He's a cool guy with a great personality. His name is Kenny. He restocks the refrigerators every day. He's been at the school more than twenty years. Her name is May. She works in the kitchen, and if you're really nice to her in the morning, she'll give you extra Honey Nut Cheerios. Trust me; I know. Vladimir's story is important. Kenny's story is important. May's story is important. And your story's important. Remember, every person has a name. Every name has a story. And every story matters. Don't let the fact that you went to Harvard Business School become so great that you miss out on all the people along the way who make life grand."

On many occasions, I've looked back on the fifteen or so times I visited Harvard over all those years and tried to get accepted as a student. The question on the library steps on my very first visit revealed an emptiness, a longing, to do more and be more. For years, I hoped and dreamed that someday I'd get into Harvard, and for a long time, it was a dim hope and faint dream. But I didn't give up. I knew failure wasn't final, and it certainly wasn't fatal. If I'd given in to failure at any point, I would never have learned the wealth of insights I gained from my professors, I would never have met such gifted and wonderful classmates, and I never would have gotten to know Vladimir, Kenny, and May.

Fear says, "You'll be defined by your failure."
Courage responds, "Get going. Failure isn't final."

DON'T WAIT UNTIL EVERYTHING IS JUST RIGHT.

IT WILL NEVER BE PERFECT. THERE WILL ALWAYS BE

CHALLENGES, OBSTACLES, AND LESS THAN PERFECT

CONDITIONS. SO WHAT? GET STARTED NOW.

WITH EACH STEP YOU TAKE, YOU WILL GROW STRONGER

AND STRONGER, MORE AND MORE SKILLED,

MORE AND MORE SELF-CONFIDENT,

AND MORE AND MORE SUCCESSFUL.

—Mark Victor Hansen

CHAPTER 34

A Door to the Future

Instead of living a severely restricted life, avoiding risks in the hope of avoiding failure, we need to identify the 10 seconds of insane courage to step out again. If your product fails, your application is denied, or your relationship falls apart, it hurts. There's no doubt about that. I'm not advocating stoic numbness. Feel sad, get mad, but don't let the moment ruin your life. Be bigger than that. At least one person still believes in you. Go to that person. Soak up the comfort and encouragement, and find the strength to try again—maybe try the same thing with a little more wisdom, or maybe try something completely different . . . but try something.

Many of us are afraid the people we value will stop loving us when we fail, but it's the exact opposite. The people who love us care even more when we fall flat on our faces. They don't walk away; they run toward us to throw their arms around us and tell us to give it another shot. True friends always let us into their lives, and they never let us down. So here's the deal: Do you want people to be more endeared to you? Fail miserably.

Then, when you succeed, they're absolutely thrilled because they've been with you on the whole journey. When my classmates asked me to speak at the Harvard Business School ceremony, I had more people excited for me than any other time in my life. Why? For the simple reason that the journey took so long to get there. They were as happy as I was that day. One of them said, "I hope you crush that speech. I feel like I've been on this journey with you!" And they all had been.

What would you do if you weren't afraid to fail? What relationship would you start, what product would you try to create, what sport or musical instrument would you pick up, what kind of business would you start? What if the sky really was the limit? Or let's be a little more realistic. What if the fear of failure didn't haunt your thoughts and minimize your options? What if you had only a "normal" fear of failure? Would you try something great? Of course you would.

Most people look at me and conclude I have no fear of failure, that I'm totally oblivious to it. Wrong. I have dreams that are boxed in by my fears. I'd love to be one of the few people on the planet to have stepped foot in every country in the world. It would be great. But I'm also scared. My thoughts race to the catastrophe I'd probably create: I'd lose my career, I'd get some unknown disease, or I can think of even worse outcomes if you give me a minute, but you get the idea. Everyone's mind wanders to the extremes.

I'm not afraid to dream. Yes, my fears are limitations, but I try my best to address them and overcome them. As I respond to the 10 seconds when I need insane courage, I gain more confidence in my next decisions.

When we begin to change how we think about failure, we have far more hope for the future. The shackles of fear begin to drop away, and we're willing to take more chances. Sometimes things turn out far better than we ever imagined, but usually we fail somewhere along the way. Yet with the new perspective that failure isn't final, we aren't crushed. Instead of looking back in shame or down in fear, we look up to learn lessons and ahead to new opportunities. Ask the open-ended questions, the what-ifs, and be a dreamer. Look at the lessons you've learned from past experiences, and let your confidence soar. Respond to the 10 seconds of insane courage . . . and do it now. Give life a shot and see what happens.

FAILURE SHOULD BE OUR TEACHER, NOT OUR

UNDERTAKER. FAILURE IS DELAY, NOT DEFEAT.

IT IS A TEMPORARY DETOUR, NOT A DEAD END.

FAILURE IS SOMETHING WE CAN AVOID ONLY

BY SAYING NOTHING, DOING NOTHING,

AND BEING NOTHING.

—*Denis Waitley*

10 Seconds Starts Now
ROAD TO COURAGE

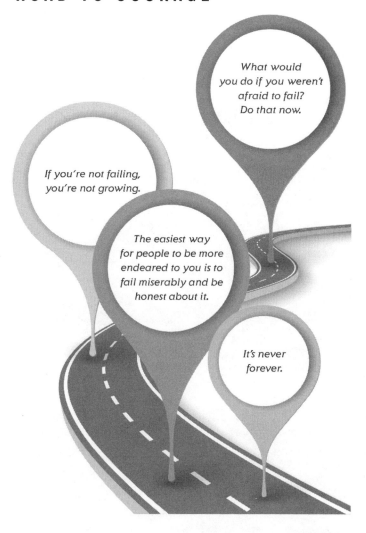

What would you do if you weren't afraid to fail? Do that now.

If you're not failing, you're not growing.

The easiest way for people to be more endeared to you is to fail miserably and be honest about it.

It's never forever.

FEAR SAYS, "YOU'LL BE DEFINED BY YOUR FAILURE."

COURAGE RESPONDS, "GET GOING. FAILURE ISN'T FINAL."

The Courage

CHAPTER 35
A Bias toward Action

CHAPTER 35

A Bias toward Action

For many of us, our fears have overwhelmed our dreams. But as we face each fear in the many moments when insane courage is required, we must act. We must become people of action, people of compassion, people of courage, and people of joy because we know our actions count. We're doing things that are no longer just about us.

A dozen times every day (maybe more often than that), we have choices. In the past, we lived in a cloud of excuses, misgivings, rationalizations, and fears. But now, we are not willing to live that way any longer.

No more procrastination. No more delays. Right now, as you're reading the words on this page, you can decide to choose courage over comfort. You know the choice. You've thought about it a million times before, and it's burning a hole in your heart at this moment. It may be about your career, your marriage, your kids, your dream of starting a company, or investing some of your considerable resources to care for people who can never pay you back.

In the next 10 seconds, you can decide to do something different. You can say "yes" to an opportunity or say "no" to that demanding person. You can write that letter to the person who needs to know you care. You can send the proposal of your great idea or submit the application to open the door to the next phase of your life. Call this person. Stop listening to that person. You can stop the behavior that's crippling you. You can start the new habit that builds you up and impacts others. Listen to the voice inside you, and do something about it. Your time is now.

A NEW YOU

In this moment, choose to do one thing different. Do it today. Eric Roth, author of the screenplay for *The Curious Case of Benjamin Button,* knew that courage was the cornerstone of living your best life. In the movie, the narrator reads Button's letter to his daughter:

> For what it's worth: it's never too late or, in my case, too early to be whoever you want to be. There's no time limit, stop whenever you want. You can change or stay the same, there are no rules to this thing. We can make the best or the worst of it. I hope you make the best of it. And I hope you see things that startle you. I hope you feel things you never felt before. I hope you meet people with a different point of view. I hope you live a life you're proud of. And if you find that you're not, I hope you have the courage to start all over again.

I would simply add: I hope you find those 10 seconds of insane courage . . . to start now.

Endnotes

1 Since I've been using this concept, a few people have asked if I got it from Matt Damon's character, Benjamin Mee, in *We Bought a Zoo*. He said, "You know, sometimes all you need is twenty seconds of insane courage. Just literally twenty seconds of just embarrassing bravery, and I promise you, something great will come of it." It's a great quote, but I think twenty seconds is stalling way too long!

2 John Levy, *The 2 AM Principle: Discover the Science of Adventure* (New York: Regan Arts, 2016), pp. 17-18.

3 Lecture by Rollo May at Sonoma State University, http://www.sonoma.edu/users/d/daniels/Maylect.html

4 Cognitive behavioral therapy addresses the complex nature of human life: emotions, beliefs, behaviors, and relationships. CBT was originally developed by Dr. Aaron Beck. One of its most effective variations is "schema therapy," which is explained by Jeffrey E. Young, Ph.D., and Janet S. Klosko, Ph.D., in their book, *Reinventing Your Life*. They identify eleven powerful, controlling belief systems that keep people stuck in unhealthy but seemingly rational perceptions of reality. They call these belief systems "lifetraps." They define and describe the concept: "A lifetrap is a pattern that starts in childhood and reverberates throughout life. It began with something that was *done* to us by our families or by other children. We were abandoned, criticized, overprotected, abused, excluded, or deprived—we were damaged in some way. Eventually the lifetrap becomes part of us. Long after we leave the home we grew up in, we continue to create situations in which we are mistreated, ignored, put down, or controlled and in which we fail to reach our most desired goals. Lifetraps determine how we think, feel, act, and relate to others. They trigger strong feelings such as anger, sadness, and anxiety. Even when we *appear* to have everything—social status, an ideal marriage, the respect of people

close to us, career success—we are often unable to savor life and believe in our accomplishments." (Young and Klesko, *Reinventing Your Life*, pp. 1-2.) The therapeutic model of schema therapy helps people clearly identify the web of false beliefs that has kept them stuck, focus on liberating truths, make choices that create a new normal, and apply these principles in a supportive environment.

5   Jeffrey E. Young and Janet S. Klosko, *Reinventing Your Life* (New York: Penguin Books, 1994), p. 6.

6   Quoted and paraphrased from "Will Smith on Skydiving," YouTube, https://www.youtube.com/watch?v=NZ-O3WEMtAE

7   "The Key to Making New Year's Resolutions Stick," Francesca Gino, *Harvard Business Review*, December 31, 2013, https://hbr. org/2013/12/the-key-to-making-new-years-resolutions-stick

8   Gayle King's interview with Dave Chappelle: https://www.you-tube.com/watch?v=GAwDds71f5g The nature show Chappelle saw: "The Thirsty Baboon," https://www.youtube.com/watch?v=YAy8LUmXPmo

9   To see a video of when I took some friends back to the orphan-age to visit Martin and the other children, go to https://www. youtube.com/watch?v=pwCvQw7sWAk

10 "The Greatest Garage Inventions of All Time," Nicole Dieker, March 6, 2015, http://www.sparknotes.com/mindhut/2015/03/06/the-greatest-garage-inventions-of-all-time

11 "Elon Musk's Risky Business," Gary Rivlin, *Men's Journal*, http://www.mensjournal.com/magazine/elon-musk-s-risky-business-20120803

12 "Sheryl Sandberg: 'I Dread Father's Day,'" Diane Tsai and Belinda Luscombe, *Time*, April 24, 2017, http://time.com/4751055/sheryl-sandberg-fathers-day/?xid=homepage

13 "The Misfit," Lynn Hirshberg, *Vanity Fair*, April 1991, Vol. 54, Issue 4, pp.160-169, 196-202.

14 video.search.yahoo.com/yhs/search?fr=yhs-GenieoYaho-fh_
   ds&hsimp=yhs-fh_ds&hspart=GenieoYaho&p=Brad+Cohen+to-
   urette+syndrome#id=4&vid=87e5826508d211320229f28cbf8c-
   1b53&action=click

   Brad Cohen is the author with Lisa Wysocky of *Front of the Class:
   How Tourette Syndrome Made Me the Teacher I Never Had* (New
   York: St. Martin's Griffin, 2008).

15 "Try Everything," Shakira, writers Sia Kate Furler, Tor
   Hermansen, Mikkel Storleer Eriksen, from the movie, *Zootopia*,
   Walt Disney Animation Studios, 2016, Published by: Lyrics ©
   Walt Disney Music Company.

16 "The Rock Is Dead. Long Live Dwayne Johnson, American
   Treasure," Scott Raab, *Esquire*, June 29, 2015, http://
   www.esquire.com/entertainment/interviews/a36037/
   dwayne-johnson-the-rock-0815/

17 "Why Wait? The Psychological Origins of Procrastination," Elliott
   T. Berkman, Ph.D., *Psychology Today*, October 8, 2015, https://
   www.psychologytoday.com/blog/the-motivated-brain/201510/
   why-wait-the-psychological-origins-procrastination

18 "'Cap Over Wall' Joined Political Lexicon," Letter to the editor
   by Clifton A. Leonhardt, *The New York Times*, February 19, 1996,
   http://www.nytimes.com/1996/02/19/opinion/l-cap-over-wall-
   joined-political-lexicon-055735.html

19 "The CEO of a multi-million dollar company explains what he
   did in his 20s to set himself up for success in his 30s," Libby Kane
   and Alyson Shontell, *Business Insider*, May 4, 2017, http://www.
   businessinsider.com/how-gary-vaynerchuk-set-himself-up-for-
   success-in-his-30s-2017-5

20 Gary Vaynerchuk, *Crush It!* (New York: HarperCollins, 2009),
   p. 3.

21 https://www.garyvaynerchuk.com/tag/daily-vlog/

22 Gary Vaynerchuk, *Jab, Jab, Jab, Right Hook* (New York:
   HarperCollins, 2003), p. 6.

23 "90% of Startups Fail: Here's What You Need to Know about the 10%," Neil Patel, *Forbes*, January 16, 2015, https://www.forbes.com/sites/neilpatel/2015/01/16/90-of-startups-will-fail-heres-what-you-need-to-know-about-the-10/#4d6094fd6679

24 www.youtube.com/watch?v=ljqra3BcqWM Willink is the author with Leif Babin of *Extreme Ownership: How U.S. Navy Seals Lead and Win* (New York: McMillan, 2015).

25 Angela Duckworth, *Grit: The Power of Passion and Perseverance* (New York: Scribner, 2016), p. 86.

26 "A Milli Billi Trilli," 2 Chainz, Trapavelli Tre, https://genius.com/2-chainz-a-milli-billi-trilli-lyrics

27 "This Is Water," David Foster Wallace, Kenyon College, May 21, 2005, web.ics.purdue.edu/~drkelly/DFWKenyonAddress2005.pdf

28 C.S. Lewis, *Mere Christianity* (New York: HarperOne, 1951), pp. 121-122.

29 Henri Nouwen, *Life of the Beloved* (New York: Crossroad Publishing, 2002), p. 138.

30 www.youtube.com/watch?v=tHejgccKiIA

31 Dale Wimbrow, "The Guy in the Glass," 1934, http://www.the-guyintheglass.com/gig.htm

32 Kent M. Keith, *Anyway: The Paradoxical Commandments* (New York: G.P. Putnam's Sons, 2001).

33 "Oscars 2014: Read Matthew McConaughey's Very McConaughey Oscar Speech," E. Alex Jung, March 3, 2014, http://www.vulture.com/2014/03/read-mcconaugheys-very-mc-conaughey-oscar-speech.html

34 "The Sermon Notes," Andy Stanley—Leadercast 2014, http://www.thesermonnotes.com/andy-stanley-leadercast-2014/

35 "Sara Blakely, Spanx: My First Million," Lauren Drell, *The Huffington Post*, March 9, 2012, http://www.huffingtonpost.com/2011/02/13/sara-blakely-spanx_n_908669.html

36 "If You're Not Failing, You're Not Growing," Ron Friedman, 99U, http://99u.com/articles/37669/if-youre-not-failing-youre-not-growing

37 "What is Catastrophizing? Cognitive Distortions," Alice Boyes, Ph.D., *Psychology Today*, https://www.psychologytoday.com/blog/in-practice/201301/what-is-catastrophizing-cognitive-distortions

38 "29 famous people who failed before they succeeded," Rachel Sugar, Richard Feloni, and Ashley Lutz, *Business Insider*, July 9, 2015, http://www.businessinsider.com/successful-people-who-failed-at-first-2015-7/#lt-

39 Quoted by H. Jackson Brown in *P.S. I Love You: When Mom Wrote, She Always Saved the Best for Last* (Nashville: Rutledge Hill Press, 1990), p. 13.

Acknowledgements

A+ PARENTS AND FAMILY

I would like to thank my Dad, my Mom, my brother Jeff and his wife Becca. A big thanks to our family glue, my Aunt Sharon, as well as Uncle Bob, Jason, Ian and all of our extended family. You each have made me the man I am today. Also, to my Dad who couldn't be here today—I hope I continue to make you proud and live a life in your legacy. To my brother Jeff—I hope you know that you always make me proud. I'm amazed at all you've accomplished and how you continue to do it with humility. To his wife Becca—you are fantastic. I'm so happy to have you as part of the family and for including me for so long as a third wheel. And lastly, to my Mom—I love our Wednesday lunches and can't thank you enough for how great you truly are.

ACADEMIC MENTORS:

UGA—Thank you to Vince Dooley, Barbara Dooley, (Deanna & all the Dooleys) and Coach Mark Richt for your unwavering support and getting involved from the very beginning. Also to President Jere Morehead, Victor Wilson, and Melenie Lankau. Thank you for getting me through the greatest school ever: The University of Georgia. Go Dawgs!

Harvard Business School—Lisa Hughes, Prof. Rohit Deshpande, Prof. Amy Cuddy, Prof. Gary Pisano, Prof. Anita Elberse and others. Thank you for helping a lifelong dream come true and for putting up with my suits, stories, and nostalgia for the South. PS: Thanks to admissions as well . . . it took 15 years, but you finally let me in.

CHICK-FIL-A MENTORS

I would like to thank David Salyers and Rodney Bullard for supporting Chick-fil-A Leader Academy and believing in the Chick-fil-A Fellows program. You guys are pioneers, mentors, and amazing leaders. Also, a huge thanks to L.J. Yankosky, John Mattioli, Tim Tassopoulos, John Stephenson, and the Cathy family for running a wonderful company based on the values of servant leadership.

ENTREPRENEURIAL ENDEAVORS

H.E.R.O. for Children—Thank you to my co-founder Ryan Gembala and all of our H.E.R.O. staff, volunteers, and board members. What a journey it has been! One of the greatest adventures of my life was helping start this and seeing how it has taken off with the support of so many.

UGA HEROs—"If it's not WOW, it's not worth doing!" I love this organization and the swag that we continue to have in supporting our kids. Keep up the great work and keep thinking big, bold and daring in our approach to raising funds and making a difference.

Global L.E.A.D.—Thank you to my co-founder Robbie Reese and our original cast of conspirators to make it all possible: Courtney Doran and Kevin Scott. Also, a huge thank you to Jesse Peel you for your unwavering faith and friendship. Not only have you supported all of my endeavors; you were the first one to be there.

ADDO Worldwide—Thank you to my co-founder Kevin Scott and to all of our co-workers. From being awarded the New Company of the Year in the state of Georgia to winning Best Places to Work, it truly has been a great ride. Also, our ADDO Ambassadors. There are too many to count, but just know Hemingway would be proud of each and every one of you. Also, a big thanks to the ADDO non-profit board members: Josh Paradis, Matt Elliot, and David Nicholas.

FRIENDS, SUPPORTERS, CONFIDANTES

Jon Vaughan and Kevin Scott—Big thanks, gentlemen, for being two friends that have known me the longest and know me the best. From Wheeler High and student government to UGA HEROs and dropping toy cows out of a helicopter, it's been real, fellas! Also to Travis Canova and Will Childs—I can't thank you enough for your friendship and ridiculous stories. From HOA and Sig Ep, to Herman Cain International and incredible snake outs . . . it's always a blast.

Grant Zarzour and Old School UGA HEROs—This is a thank you for 15 years of UGA HEROs. From our glory days dropping cows out of helicopters to winning Organization of the Year, and Best Campus Event. A special thanks to Grant Zarzour, Brie Zarzour, (and Kelsey Vinson) for our work in Antarctica and Athens, GA along with all the amazing people over the years.

HARVARD OF ATHENS

Standing ovation for Travis Canova, Will Childs, Tim Mcnary, Satya Patel, Latham Saddler, Miles Garrison, Nipul & Nitin Patel, Justin Golshir, Bryan Lassiter, and my co-founder Jon Ostenson.

HUGE THANK YOU

And a final big thank you to every friend, mentor, colleague, and supporter along the way. First, a special thanks to my favorite Brazilian, Rosane Rezende—You are the best amore! Thank you, Chi Chi Patrick, Travis D, Kameko, and the entire Push It Up party, the ATL entrepreneur squad, my 7B Living Group at HBS and Kevin Swiss for our work on The Dash. Thank you to Dan Lack, Mitali Chakraborty, and Gina Rudan for always pushing me to dream big. Friends for life Brooks Bradway, Jessica Grant, Eric Brown, Taylor Jones, and Dan Duncan. Also, Phil Minnes and JCI International, the Brozen crew, Drew Fulton and Tory, Blake Canterbury, David Nicholas, Britton Clark, Caleb Jones, Adam Boyle, and Andrew Dill. Our Chick-fil-A colleagues, Jessica Purser and Matt Lingerfelt. Our Chick-fil-A Leader Academy team of Laura Engelbrecht, Jackie Staley, Elizabeth Jay, Linda Cottrell, Patrick McConn, and Rosy Harvey. The Omar crew to Cuba—Erin Perez, Blake Morris, and John Hightower. The international crew from AIESEC Romania, Stuart and Sam from Australia, and Pastor Paulus from Indonesia. And lastly, thanks to Doug Schwartz for all our travel and adventures.

WRITING | EDITING MENTORS:

To Pat Springle, Josh Paradis, and Josh Plemmons. Thank you, Pat, for your vision and care when it came to capturing the heart of this book and all the endless rounds of edits. You are truly gifted, and I can't thank you enough for helping make this a reality. Thank you to Mr. Paradis for re-imagining this book from that train ride through Romania years ago to now, it's been quite the journey. And Mr. Plemmons, thank you for your comedy gold and clever handle of the human language. Your ExtraGuacBlog. com was a true inspiration for my writing.

To everyone, I'm forever grateful.

About ADDO

ADDO WORLDWIDE

ADDO is Latin for "inspire." Garrett Gravesen is the co-founder of both ADDO Institute and ADDO Worldwide along with his business partner Kevin Scott. ADDO Worldwide, LLC is a leadership consulting firm with a mission to engage, expose, and equip leaders at all levels around the world. ADDO consults on strategic business initiatives, communication strategies, and leadership development programs. To learn more visit www.ADDO.is

ADDO CO-FOUNDERS GARRETT GRAVESEN AND KEVIN SCOTT WITH FORMER SECRETARIES OF STATE COLIN POWELL, JAMES BAKER, WARREN CHRISTOPHER, MADELEINE ALBRIGHT, AND HENRY KISSINGER

The Road to 196

Garrett Gravesen is on a mission to visit all 196 countries. 22 people alive have ever done it. Part Anthony Bourdain *Parts Unknown*, part Jim Carrey *Yes Man*, Gravesen will capture stories and circumstances of people saying YES as they face 10 seconds of insane courage. After studying human behavior and leadership development at Harvard Business School, Garrett is heading outside the classroom and corporate boardroom to re-discover the elements of insane courage to face fear, overcome obstacles, and live an extraordinary life.

Follow along as Garrett chronicles the journey, shares the stories, and uncovers the leadership lessons from remote places around the world. To follow the journey, share an idea, or perhaps be included, visit GarrettGravesen.com

More Courage

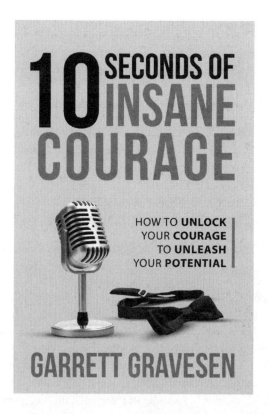

For more information or to order more copies of this book
go to garrettgravesen.com

More Comments about
10 Seconds of Insane Courage...

If America's zeitgeist is fear, then Garrett Gravesen is the antidote. He names and then demystifies the things that stand between us and living the lives we dream about. I urge you to read his book.
— **David Metcalf, Spencer Stuart Leadership Advisory Services**

Garrett has never fit in any boxes, and in his debut book, he masterfully articulates how to face your fears and beat indecision. Fear is the most significant barrier we face in our life journeys, but on the other side of our fear we often discover the best things in life. So much can happen in a 10-second decision, and your choice to read this book is one of them.
— **Eric Brown, Co-founder & CCO, Whiteboard**

Finally, a book that speaks directly to society's common problem, FEAR, and how to overcome it with COURAGE. When Garrett talks (or in this case writes), you should listen. Pay attention to this one!
— **Matt Shanks, AmWINS Brokerage**

This book has encouragement we all need and advice that you'll apply immediately. Garrett is the perfect person to write this because his communication style and life stories can only be summed up by "wow!" Start reading it today, your life will be better instantly.
— **Blake Canterbury, Founder of Purposity, finding purpose through generosity**

From the life experiences of a fantastic motivator and storyteller, the lessons in this book rocked my world and led me to choose courage over comfort in all aspects of my life.
— **Matt Thomas, Founder, Brawl for a Cause**

Garrett, a college classmate and fraternity brother, always challenged me to take the great risk and make the hard choice. Thankfully for all of us, he has heeded his own advice in writing this great exhortation. I look forward to accepting his next challenge.
— **Travis Canova, The Accountant**

Garrett is a man of his word, a man of grand gestures, surprises, humor, hard work, adventure and generosity. He is a man who practices what he preaches. That's Garrett—he lives his life by the words he writes, and he is a happier, more fulfilled person because of it. He lives by his belief that it only takes 10 seconds of insane courage to live an inspired life. If you ever wanted to do something but felt you couldn't, if you ever wanted to try something but allowed your fear to stand in your way, read this book. You'll be inspired to go for it and not ask "why?", but "why not?"
— **Rosane Rezende, Special Agent**

I told Garrett not to write this book because 10 seconds later everyone would have conquered their fears and he'd have nothing left to do.
— **Josh Plemmons, Green Bank**

Having first-hand experience for close to 25 years in our friendship, I am fortunate to have a unique perspective on Garrett's connection to facing fear and being both insane and courageous in the face of that fear. From girls and student government to college life and politics to starting new non-profit ventures and ultimately facing the final days with his father, I have been privileged to see Garrett face fear over and over again. He is insane, there's no doubt, but the courage he has shown in the face of these fears makes his story real and inspiring. This is not an idea born out of research, but rather, one built out of experience, I know you will enjoy it and learn from it.
— **Jon Vaughan, President, Brand Vaughan Lumber Company**

Garrett's ability to tell stories that inspire you to do more and be more borders on pure genius. This is his unique talent. So, it's a gift to have his creative and intelligent take on "courage vs. fear" published for the world to read. Extremely visionary to say the least.
— **Kevin M Swiss, Senior Creative Director, Vivint Smart Home Inc.**

I know Garrett from the Harvard Business School leadership program we undertook together. In many of the business cases, program activities and social events, at one point we all displayed different fears. Garrett was no exception. The difference was how confident he was about facing them. His amazing life story for doing what he does and what he'd learn in the process really allowed him to tackle fear with a whole different perspective. I can't wait for everyone to learn the key lessons from this brand-new book
— **Javier Thames, Grupo Coel**